This caregiver's guide is so muc Cording *weaves in personal anecdotes of her own caregiver journey, star-studded interviews, and yes, even music playlists. This framework makes it an interesting read that's also chock-full of tips to help you take care of yourself so you can show up better for those you're tending to.*

—Samantha Cassetty, MS, RD,
nutrition and wellness expert and co-author of *Sugar Shock*

This is an important resource for caregivers of all kinds. Jess's engaging combination of storytelling, actionable tips, and mind-body wellness insight makes this an approachable, relatable tool for the overwhelmed caregiver.

—Jason Wachob, Founder & Co-CEO, mindbodygreen

I know all too well how difficult caregiving can be and this book, which blends approachable advice, personal story, and even a playlist, is an essential tool to help avoid or recover from burnout. You'll learn the basics of what to eat to keep your energy and mood up, how to improve sleep, make movement part of your life even with minimal time, and more. No matter where on your journey you are, The Farewell Tour *can help lighten the load.*

—Max Lugavere,
NY Times Best-selling author, science journalist, and podcast host

Jessica Cording has utilized the best of her massive talents as a storyteller, interviewer, and dietitian/health coach to create this extraordinary book that I know I will continue to pick up and read for years to come.

—Adam Wade,
20-Time Moth StorySlam Winner and
Author of *You Ought to Know Adam Wade*

The Farewell Tour *is so much MORE than a book— it's a guide-post for anyone, anywhere who is (or will become) a caregiver. It's truly THE book that I so desperately wanted to read (and searched for to no avail!) when my dad was sick, and I laughed, cried, and yelped affirmations aloud as I devoured it start-to-finish in an afternoon. Jess is as masterful at writing and story-telling as she is at applying science-based evidence to her patients' real lives as a health practitioner. Yes, this book is filled with compassion, love, humor, resilience, and grief; but it's also an exceptionally practical guide that provides tangible, actionable strategies that can help make life less difficult so that you can make the most of the time you have with the people you love.*

—Jaclyn London, MS, RD, CDN,
Consultant, Brand/Media Expert, and Author of *Dressing on the Side (and Other Diet Myths Debunked): 11 Science-Based Ways to Eat More, Stress Less, and Feel Great About Your Body.*

The Farewell Tour *is a life resource tool that the entire world could use right now—not just caregivers. Clever and heart-warming, illuminating and raw, Jessica shares her expert ingredients and soundtrack for a well-lived life.*

—Kate Eckman,
award-winning author of *The Full Spirit Workout*

the farewell tour

the farewell tour

*A Caregiver's Guide to Stress Management,
Sane Nutrition, and Better Sleep*

Jessica Cording, MS, RD, CDN, INHC

This book is dedicated to my family.
Thanks for always making the best road trip playlists.

Published in the United States by Viva Editions, an imprint of Start Midnight, LLC, 221 River Street, Ninth Floor, Hoboken, New Jersey 07030.

Printed in the United States
Cover design: Jennifer Do
Cover image: Shutterstock
Text design: Frank Wiedemann

First Edition.
10 9 8 7 6 5 4 3 2 1

Trade paper ISBN: 978-1-63228-075-6
E-book ISBN: 978-1-63228-132-6

TABLE OF CONTENTS

INTRODUCTION

While nutrition and wellness are my professional passions, writing and music have always kept me moving forward. I usually have a song in my head and a soundtrack for pretty much everything. When I started on my career path as a dietitian and health coach, I knew in my gut that somewhere along the way, writing and music would find their way into the story somehow, and it's certainly been an interesting trail of crumbs to follow.

A core part of my writing work has always been to create resources I wish I'd had when I needed them. Sometimes that has been a resource for patients and clients, and in some cases, something I could have used for my own needs.

This book is intended to be a resource for caregivers of all types—not just those caring for someone with a terminal illness, though that was how it started. As a dietitian in an ALS clinic early in my career, I got to know my patients and their families and saw the wear and tear the whole family went through. It was in that role where I became keenly interested in the emotional and social aspects of food as a connector and in finding ways to provide the best quality experience possible during a challenging time.

I naively had thought that my work in that area would prepare me if any of my own family members ever experienced a serious illness with a poor prognosis, but not surprisingly, I was introduced to a bunch of unanticipated struggles when it came to my own father's health journey.

When my dad was first diagnosed with advanced and inoperable pancreatic cancer, his attitude was "Well, someone has to be the first to survive this" so we dropped everything to support him. Because his prognosis was so bleak, we went into "sprint mode," so to speak, burning the candle at both ends, trying to squeeze in as much as possible while maintaining a positive exterior. At first, the trial drugs worked well (though they came with sometimes debilitating side effects) but as the months went on and the cancer stopped responding, the energy shifted. It became about making the most we could of our time together.

My father wanted to live whatever was left of his life on his terms and remain as social as possible—when he wanted to be social, that is. I walked into the kitchen one afternoon as he hung up the phone and chuckled to himself. He grabbed an ice cream bar from the freezer and mused as he unwrapped, "When they find out you're dying, everybody wants a piece of you."

So we started calling it "The Farewell Tour."

In some ways, it really did feel like being on the road, touring with a band, where my dad was the headliner, my mother the road manager, and my sister and I part of the crew with our specific duties. Because my dad had worked in the music industry, a large part of his work had involved helping organize and promote many tours, albums, and artist campaigns—it was a framework my family understood. Going to concerts all those years and seeing the joy but also the exhaustion in the eyes of the artists and crew members had stuck with me (and had a *lot* to do with why I never pursued a career in the entertainment industry). There were even times when younger artists stayed at my parents' house when they were playing New York, and I remember the suitcases and the vans and buses parked wherever they would fit and what a relief a home-cooked meal could be after weeks of fast food.

For the fifteen months my dad battled his disease, I never once fully unpacked my overnight bag. I even got to know the different drivers on the bus route I took between New York City and New Jersey at least once a week. As the dietitian of the family, I made it my job to see that everyone ate well when I was around. In retrospect, I'm not totally sure my help was welcome or if it seemed meddling, but it was at least something I could do when so much was out of my hands. My mom and I used to spend a lot of time on the phone discussing my dad's latest labs and what to put in his milkshakes and what to pack in the cooler she brought on chemo days.

The long days at the hospital with the constantly changing schedule of rotating doctors and nurses and the few familiar faces made me feel disoriented when I'd step out onto the sidewalk and try to interact with others. Every handout from every new provider was like a new call sheet, a new set list. It was like every time we got the hang of it, the routine changed.

I wanted to create something that would be inclusive for people supporting loved ones for whom the priority is making the best of what time they have left. I remember feeling left out when looking for caregiver resources, sometimes even like I was being made to feel guilty for thinking realistically instead of blindly hoping for a miracle. Also, was it okay to laugh? Because wow, we laughed *so much* at the darkest stuff.

While my family's story is about supporting someone going

through terminal cancer, my hope is that this book can be helpful to caregivers of all types.

I also want to note that we all process grief differently. I seem to take after my paternal grandfather, who mourned the loss of my grandma's death from stomach cancer by tinkering around the house. I accepted the offer to write *The Little Book of Game Changers* literally the day after my dad died, and many times throughout the writing process, I came back to the image of my grandfather at the top of a ladder, hammer in hand and nails between his teeth. Though I did speak with my mom and sister about their experience throughout the writing of this book, they preferred not to do formal interviews, as it was difficult for them to revisit painful memories.

Another thing I felt I should comment on: You may notice that a lot of the music artists and industry individuals I interviewed are white men of a certain age. I struggled a lot with this—I wanted to speak primarily with people with whom my dad had worked, and while he did work with some women and with people of color, at the time he was most active in his industry, rock and roll was really, really white—and male-dominated. I labored over how best to address this imbalance in these pages. Between the artists and health experts I interviewed for this book, I did my best to feature a variety of voices as I do in all my writing, but I always keep an eye on how I can do better. Because this book is part "how-to" and part storytelling, I view these artist interviews as part of the "story." These individuals are sharing their unique experience of touring with a band, but exactly that: unique to that person and not reflective of all artists and music industry professionals.

You'll see "suggested listening" in each chapter. I pulled from Spotify playlists my dad and I both had made during his illness and added them in where they fit. Playlists are my family's love language, and it helped me write this book. Feel free to listen along.

So whether you are caring for a friend or family member, are a professional caregiver in some capacity, or are simply interested in learning about how to take care of yourself while supporting others, I hope you find this book to be a useful resource.

CHAPTER 1

BEST-CASE SCENARIO

When I got the call, I was on my way to break up with my therapist.

Both my parents were on speakerphone. "I don't know how else to say this," my mom started, "so I'm just going to say it."

I remember feeling like I already knew what she was going to tell me.

"It looks like your father has pancreatic cancer."

I thought back a few weeks to when we'd last had dinner together. A couple bites in, my father had pushed his plate away with a puzzled, upset look on his face. "Something's just not right," he'd said. He'd been back and forth to a few different doctors over the past month, trying antibiotics, talking about changing his diet (for real this time), and while he'd initially rolled his eyes at the urgent care doctor who'd written a prescription for a CAT scan, I think he knew too.

I stood there with my phone to my ear, trying to gather my thoughts, knowing that I couldn't stall much longer without it being awkward. So I just opened my mouth and hoped for the best: "I am so, so sorry."

Sorry? I said to myself. *Sorry is the best you can do? What's wrong with you?* Or was I being too hard on myself? I didn't recognize it in the moment, but it was the same mechanism in my brain that kicked in when I had to show up to work and see patients during Hurricane Sandy in 2012, and the one that later enabled me to counsel ALS patients without crying when I talked with them about initiating tube feeding.

If my parents found my response dissatisfying, they didn't say so. We quickly fell into making arrangements for me to get out to their house in New Jersey that evening so we could talk about it in person.

Surprisingly, my therapist didn't charge me for the missed session. Even though I'd felt like I had hit a wall in my eight years of working with her (I'd started when I was twenty-three, and so much had changed since then), I'd decided I wouldn't stop my treatment yet—this seemed like a bad time to change horses. She knew all about the complex relationship I had with my family, especially my dad, with whom I would often butt heads because we were so similar. While we'd been able to find a more peaceful flow in recent years, I suspected his illness would bring up lots of stuff and that maybe it would be helpful to be able to talk to someone who knew all that history.

I was the first to arrive that night. My mom filled me in that they'd told my sister's fiancé, Theo, but not my sister. Even though she's not even two years younger, my mom had always shielded Julia and tried to soften and smooth what she could for her. I'm the crispy test-pancake child who can do stoic pretty well.

My dad was kneeling on the floor with the dog as he calmly broke the news that the doctors had found what they believed to be pancreatic cancer and that later that week, he was going to meet his oncology team and talk about next steps. While it didn't look good, he was going to fight it, and he was happy we could all be together.

Theo, who at 6'2" towered over my dad by almost a foot, reached down and hugged him. "I love you, Jim." Since I was barely ever home, it was the first time it really clicked for me that Theo truly had become a part of the family. Had I really been that tuned out?

At that point in my life, I was juggling a per diem hospital job, a weekly corporate wellness gig, private coaching clients, and regular speaking engagements, not to mention enough writing assignments that I needed to keep a monthly calendar of deadlines. I filled my free time with networking meetings and conferences. As a result, I rarely saw my friends or family, and had started joking about being on an "extended hiatus" from dating. I was thirty-one and watching everyone around me pair off (including, yes, my younger sister—birth order was the first question anyone ever asked when I mentioned she was getting married), but after a string of disappointments, I had chosen to channel my energy into my career. I was, essentially, the real-life embodiment of the Hallmark Movie "Career Girl" archetype, the one who hates Christmas and keeps her visits to her hometown as short as possible.

When it came up in conversation that I was a single woman in my thirties living and working and writing in Manhattan, inevitably someone would say, "Like *Sex & The City*!" I'd usually say something like, "Sure, if Carrie Bradshaw wore a lab coat and custom orthotics!" The truth was, though, I hadn't so much as been on a date in a year.

As I went to bed that night in my old bedroom at my parents' house, I thought of all the moving pieces of my personal and professional life. *So. Many. Pieces.* So many spreadsheets and calendars and calculations. And what was it adding up to? There was no way I could keep it all up at the pace I had been and still be present for my family. My dad had made it very clear that he considered us all on this cancer journey together—and I wanted to be there. A lot would have to change.

The next morning, I had to go back to the city for an appointment, so I was up early to work out and pack up. As I was making breakfast in the kitchen, my dad came in. It was the first time we'd been alone since I'd been back.

"Want some eggs and sweet potato?" I offered.

"No thanks. I went to the bakery." He grabbed a plate and sat down at the table. He reached into the brown paper bag he'd brought in. "They tell me I have cancer," he said, "so I'm going to eat this fucking donut *and* this buttered roll."

We didn't talk much as we ate—I wasn't sure where to start— but we naturally began discussing his upcoming appointment and the logistics and what he expected would take place. I think he was hoping that a doctor would come in and say, "I looked at the films again—we messed up. You're fine!" We all wanted that.

As we loaded our plates into the dishwasher, I said, "Well, worst-case scenario, you have something so rare, they name it after you."

He thought this over for a moment and then chuckled. "That actually sounds like best-case scenario," he said. "I've always wanted to be remembered."

Three days later we met at the hospital in the city to learn more about the bizarre journey we were about to embark on.

"So, the pancreas is shaped kind of like a hot dog."

The oncologist held up a picture and started pointing as he explained the location of the tumor and why surgery was not a viable option for my father.

My family nodded along, trying to take it all in. I just kept thinking, "Well, I'm never going to be able to look at a hot dog the same way again." Honestly, though, no love lost there.

A few hours later, when we had finished meeting with a few other members of my dad's new care team and it was time to take a break for lunch between appointments, he said, without a hint of irony, "I could really go for a hot dog."

CHAPTER 2

A LITTLE FAMILY HISTORY

Suggested Listening: "I'm From New Jersey"
—JOHN GORKA

"Teach Your Children"
—CROSBY, STILLS, NASH & YOUNG

My dad, James "Rocky" Del Balzo Jr., grew up working class in Long Island, New York. Despite his Greek-Italian heritage, he had a big head of curly red hair. My grandparents both worked multiple jobs and bred and showed dogs as their weekend hobby. My dad grew up scooping up dog poop and worked in an animal hospital all through high school. When I was an animal-obsessed kid, I used to beg him to tell me stories about his furry and feathered patients.

Always an athlete, my dad was scouted for minor league baseball, but at 5'5", was deemed too short, so he went to college, thinking he'd become a veterinarian. He quickly learned that veterinary school was not his destiny, so he switched to communications, intending to go into sportscasting—he had a unique voice that was perfect for radio. Along the way, he fell into music, hanging posters until he worked his way up to a position at a record label in New York, reaching out to college stations.

My parents met when my mother was a program director at her school's music station, and they developed a professional friendship. As the story goes, that changed when he invited her to attend a press junket in New York for The Jam and asked her to come to lunch with the group. They were both super young and my mom wasn't looking to meet anybody, but she'd later say that when he kissed her on the cheek as they said goodbye that day, her knees buckled a little.

My parents got married a month after my mom finished college. They moved to LA, which they hated so much, they moved as quickly as possible back to the East Coast. My sister and I came along a few years later. My parents worked very hard at their respective jobs, so while we were "comfortable," financially, we lived in an area where our friends lived in giant mansions and took fabulous ski vacations and traveled to private islands. My parents were always quick with a reality check about their own upbringing to point out how lucky we were so we wouldn't lose perspective.

Honestly, though, growing up, I never would have traded with my friends who flew first class. Sure, I guess it would have been cool to go on exotic trips, but even as a child, I kind of hated the beach (I'm terrified of the ocean and sunburn easily), and the idea of zooming down a mountain through the snow sounded like a combination of a few of my least favorite things, so I didn't feel like I was missing out. Besides, I got to tag along to concerts and hang out backstage, watching the show from the wings where I could see all the behind-the-scenes stuff. I was an observant, quiet kid, taught from an early age to play it cool and stay out of the way, and I soaked it all in like a sponge.

My dad worked in promotions, and for most of my life, was at Columbia records, eventually becoming Senior Vice President of Promotions. He did a brief stint at MTV when it was still in its infancy, but his friend and former boss Paul Rappaport brought him back into the Columbia / Sony Music fold. It was a demanding but creative job that allowed him to use his passion for music, people skills, and fearlessness to get his artists' records played. It was a point of pride for him that he did so without greasing the wheels via gifting DJs cocaine, a standard practice at the time. I learned all my best curse words on Take Your Daughter to Work Day. The office had a certain buzz to it, and I loved the electricity of the shows, even though I also saw the nonglamorous side too.

While I saw mostly how hard my dad worked (and the crazy hours and travel required), we did get to do some cool stuff too. The concerts, of course, were a major perk, and as a kid I loved sitting in on press conferences and watching the exchange between the journalists and artists, flashbulbs going off all over the place. We also got to tag along sometimes on other promotional events. One that sticks out to me was a promo for Pink Floyd's 1994 album, *The Division Bell*. During the tour Columbia records flew a 194-foot airship (dubbed *The Division Belle*) between tour locations. When the zeppelin came to the Tri-State Area, my dad brought my mom, sister, and I on board for a ride with some local contest winners. I've always been a little afraid of heights, but even I was dazzled by the view.

My dad left Columbia in 2002 to do his own thing. It felt like the right time for him to pivot. The industry was changing quickly, thanks to streaming music, in a way that made it seem like the rug was being pulled out from under the machines. For the next sixteen years, he did consulting work and managed established and emerging artists. You'll see a few of those names in these pages. In writing this book and talking to various artists and industry people, I came to understand my dad in a different way. I knew who he was at home, and I knew how deeply passionate he was about music and how loyal he was to those he worked with, but it was a revelation to hear stories about the force of nature he was.

Everyone I interviewed for this book remarked at how refreshingly down to earth and humble and irreverently funny my dad was. They also spoke of his love of the music, uncommon in an industry where the business side has been notoriously disconnected from the craft. To come across someone who enjoyed the creation of the music within the context of making it commercially viable was rare, they said.

My dad would blast whatever he was interested in or working on at the time to the point where the house shook. He was constantly making us mix CDs and later, playlists. My mom played us her favorite albums in the car. I still think of various phases of my life in terms of, say, *Revolver* summer, *Tapestry* spring, and *After the Gold Rush* October. Every phase has its soundtrack.

To be totally honest, I was nervous about including details about my dad's work in this book, scared of giving anyone the wrong idea about my family. Even though we were aware of the glamorous side, there was a very clear understanding that this stuff was a *job*. Much of our together time as a family revolved around my dad's work—the vacations we did go on usually took place where my dad was traveling to for a conference or where one of his artists had a show. When I sat down to write about my dad's "Farewell Tour" (or as I'll call it in some parts, the Cancer Tour or the Cancer Show), I realized I couldn't not talk about his work—it was so important to him and such a central part of my own upbringing.

What you see in these pages is just the small sliver I had room to share. I was blown away by the generosity of the people who shared their time, insight, and stories with me for this book. In my head, in so many ways, I still feel like that little girl sitting on an amp watching an artist strum away and sing out into the bright lights of yet another venue, giving it their all.

CHAPTER 3

WHAT'S IN YOUR BAG?

Suggested Listening: "New Amsterdam"
—ELVIS COSTELLO & THE ATTRACTIONS

The first time I ever packed a "go bag" was during Hurricane Sandy in 2012 when I was living in NYC and doing my dietetic internship at NewYork-Presbyterian Hospital. I was up at the Columbia campus in Washington Heights, and during that week, rather than continue with my pediatric rotation, I was tossed into staff relief on whatever floors needed dietitian coverage. I also did a few shifts serving food from our emergency supply in the cafeteria. It was controlled chaos, but chaos nonetheless. That first day, my heart was in my mouth the whole time. I remember feeling like I was moving at double speed.

I have a very clear memory of running up a stairwell, on my way to see patients on the sixth floor, when I nearly collided with a medical resident who was lumbering down. He sang a very slow, mournful rendition of "The Times, They Are A-Changing" at the top of his lungs. He did not even see me.

I felt something click into place in my mind. Things *were* changing. Yes, I could spend my energy being scared, or I could focus on what I had to do and put a smile on my face to help put those around me at ease. I was there to serve my patients, and right now, that meant putting my own fear aside. I recognized that this moment would stay with me. It was this tiny thing, but it felt like the beginning of the rest of my life.

So, about the go bag.

A go bag is, essentially, an emergency preparedness bag you pack ahead of time—and of course, hope you never need. It was a phrase I'd been hearing since I was a teenager, living outside New York in the days just after 9/11, when people were talking about building fallout shelters or moving off the grid far away from major cities. This idea that, at any moment, you might have to pick up and run certainly contributed to a lot of existential anxiety (on top of the usual cocktail of teenage drama), but I didn't realize how loud the echo was until my internship director was emailing us instructions about what to bring to work with us in case we had to sleep at the hospital.

It would be years until I could relax enough not to always have a toothbrush plus a spare pair of contact lenses and underwear in my purse when I just running around the city for a regular workday. When I was dating, I mastered the art of squeezing a shocking amount of "just in case" into smallish purses while still somehow leaving room for my EpiPen.

When we talk about self-care, we often talk about having the right tools in our toolbox. During very tumultuous or stressful times, however, I have found that it feels more like a backpack you carry with you—and you need to make sure you have those essentials, but not so many self-care practices that you feel weighed down by them. Learning essential self-care practices before we're in crisis mode (and hopefully never having that experience, but let's be real, the world isn't exactly getting simpler) and having those strategies already in place can help us when we do need them. While it's great to have that well-stocked toolbox, it's also okay to focus just on what feels essential for a particularly intense stretch or for each part of a long journey.

It makes me think of people who are constantly traveling for work. Because my dad had to travel a lot to places his colleagues and artists went, he was away at least a few times a month. I also remember the way the artists he worked with would talk about life on the road being different from when they were at home. This comes up for people in other professions too. As a dietitian and health coach I have worked with people in all different industries who found themselves regularly traveling for their jobs, and a central part of our work together involved coming up with some go-to healthy habits to give them some semblance of structure even when they were living out of a suitcase or going across time zones. A big one: they always kept a bag packed with the essentials (clothes, toiletries, supplements, snacks, etc.) and had a version of a healthy routine for when they're traveling and need at least a few things to anchor them.

In some ways, caring for a loved one who is on a long and difficult health journey is not that different. You're on that path with them. Even if you do go home to your own bed every night, the drain of new information, new challenges, new treatments can grind on you in a similar way. Sure, you could eat crap or drink your feelings or pump yourself full of caffeine, or you could start with a few simple habits to help you feel better. I can't stress this enough: better is still better. Don't push for "perfect."

In this book, I'll share a wide variety of self-care tools with you but know that you don't need to put every single one into practice. Start with what resonates and give yourself permission to let that change over time. You may find you're starting with a few great habits in place that allow you to feel a sense of ease in one area of your life but struggle in another. Often, as situations evolve, the shake-ups to your routine mean you need to become intentional about things that were once baked into your day-to-day life.

The toolbox is a great idea, and I do love and use that example in other contexts, but this is a unique situation where we need to travel a little lighter and simplify even more. Feel free to lean in or back off from these tools as needed and know that they'll be there when you need to come back to them.

INTERVIEW WITH
PAUL RAPPAPORT

Paul Rappaport is a fifty-year record industry veteran and former vice president of album rock promotion at Columbia Records. I've known him for, literally, my entire life, as he and my dad were close friends and colleagues for many years. Early in his career, Mr. Rappaport toured extensively with the artists he was working with and had a lot of insight to share. Here, he answers my questions about the music industry life on the road.

For people who may not be familiar, what are some of the other key people involved behind the scenes for a touring artist?
The agent is someone who books the artist and puts the tours together. The artist's manager works with the agent to decide the best venues and tour packages to fit the artist's persona and fan base. The manager also helps plan the artist's overall career path and handles the basic finances along with an accountant. The artist also has a road manager who travels with the band and who's in charge of all aspects of the day-to-day tour (travel, hotels, scheduling sound checks, etc.). Then there is the road crew

("roadies") who haul the equipment into the venue, set up the stage, the sound system, and the lights. There is someone in charge of mixing the live show from the soundboard, and also someone running the lights who is located right next to the soundman. Sometimes there are large video screens and crew members in charge of all those aspects. There are also people that fix broken equipment and techs assigned to each band member, not only to help set up their drums, guitars, keyboards, etc., but also to be there during each performance if something should break, or if a guitar player needs to switch out different guitars for certain songs. Some are solely hired as drivers. Especially for large arena acts, these people are driving huge semi-tractor-trailer trucks that require a special skill and license.

Of course, artists that are playing clubs or small theaters don't require as big a road crew and some folks double-up on tasks, but as you can see there's a lot going on behind the scenes.

What are some of the physical health challenges of touring?

Lack of sleep, fatigue, and diet come to mind immediately. Many artists not only have to play multiple shows a week, but they also can have other commitments, like local media interviews each day while they're on tour. Often television or radio interviews are done with morning shows because they have the most people watching and listening. That means an artist has to get up very early in the morning, which can be quite taxing when their work carries them late into the evenings. There are press interviews and social media interviews along with all the rest of the digital platforms that an artist has to deal with. An artist can be very busy around the clock. When schedules become packed, fatigue sets in.

With so much running around, one doesn't always have their first choice for food, so staying on a healthy diet becomes a real issue. Eating healthy on the go can be quite challenging and often eating at odd hours without a daily regimen doesn't help.

The constant pace, lack of sleep, and eating on the go, will wear you out. When you are a record company representative on the road with an artist and you are organizing the media interview schedules, making sure you get the artist back to the venue in time for a sound check, and afterwards overseeing meet-and-greets with fans, press, and radio personnel, you can easily wind up as fatigued as the artist. And like the artist, you're fighting for time just to get a decent night's sleep. All those events begin to run together and after a few days you feel like you are in one long movie.

Because you change cities and accommodations daily, the road can play tricks on you. One of the funniest things that often happened to me was, I would get up in the middle of the night to go to the bathroom, and still half asleep I'd walk smack into a wall because in my mind I was remembering the bathroom from the hotel room the night before!

When I first got into the music business, it was the late sixties, early seventies. Drugs were a big part of the culture. The rock scene was exploding with new artists who found themselves on tour for the first time. This was quite exciting, and many didn't understand how taxing life on the road could be. The accent wasn't on pacing oneself and staying healthy but on partying— sometimes endlessly. All artists weren't like this, of course, but many didn't know how to control themselves. Although the drug scene proved interesting and even mind-expanding at times, too much of anything isn't good and many artists quickly found themselves behind the eight ball while on the road.

Even for artists or music industry folks who only dabbled with drugs or still do, while they may give you a lift for a little bit, they wear your energy and immune system down very quickly, lowering your chances of staying healthy on the road.

When I was head of rock promotion for Columbia Records, I found myself on tour with many different kinds of artists. I made my own choices about how much I wanted to participate in anyone's lifestyle, but it was easy to get caught up in the excitement.

There is a difference between drug use and drug abuse, and many of us used and experimented with the popular drugs of the day in social settings. For a lot of us marijuana simply took the place of alcohol. During the mid-seventies in the music business, many of us also carried a very small vial of cocaine to use socially. It was akin to carrying a flask of whiskey during prohibition and quite acceptable for people to offer a hit to one another in a social setting.

As years progressed the drug culture waned, and by 1985 when I was working closely with your dad, all of that was pretty much behind me. Your dad I were very much focused on our careers, becoming the best rock promotion people in the business. I'm proud to say we did just that. Artists like The Rolling Stones, Pink Floyd, Billy Joel, Bruce Springsteen, Elvis Costello, James Taylor, and more, loved working with us because they knew we would deliver for them like no one else, and some became close friends of ours.

By that time artists were becoming more professional on the road as well. Yes, there was some continued partying going on, but many artists' attention turned to wellness, how to stay healthy and in good shape while touring. Some insisted that concert promoters provide healthy food backstage, and some even traveled with personal trainers.

What are some of the mental and emotional challenges?
Record people stay up late. We're not morning people. We sleep in if we can. That's just how the business works. Most of our

jobs take place during the day and can go long into the evenings attending club and concert performances. When you're in charge of the daily promotion schedule for an artist while on the road, if there is an early morning interview scheduled, just like them, you've gone to bed late and gotten up early—even earlier than them, to make sure they get to that morning radio or TV show appearance on time. You have the delicate job of letting an interviewer know when it's time to wrap up because you and the artist have to get to the next event. You have a lot of things to keep straight, not only the schedule, but travel time, figuring out traffic, finding a place for a quick lunch, working with fans and industry guests if there is a meet-and-greet at the show, etc., etc.

As lack of sleep and road fatigue kick in, you can start to lose it. Your mind can't process as fast. Because you're tired, you might not be able to communicate your thoughts as well as you do when you're sharp. This brings about stress. I am a huge perfectionist and I demand of myself that *everything* runs smoothly and goes entirely as planned or better. Sometimes you have a situation where you have to think on your feet to make something a success that is going south.

Mental stress turns into emotional stress when you're not at your best. You always want to appear sharp and retain your reputation. If you miss a beat, or make a mistake due to fatigue, if you can't speak as eloquently as you'd like, or you get a bit edgy, then you are not showing yourself in the best light. When those things happened to me, I'd get very down on myself. I'd begin to worry that people would think less of me. It's the same for an artist. If their day isn't going well, or they have a fight with their spouse, girlfriend, or boyfriend, their performance can suffer. They don't have the same positive energy as when they are feeling on top of the world. They leave the stage knowing their show was a bit off, and they hate when that happens.

Life on the road can lead to emotional challenges at home too. When you've been on the road in different cities with a whole other family so to speak, and living a completely different lifestyle with different responsibilities, it takes a moment to readjust to your home life. You've come from one world and are now reentering another. You have to readjust the balance of your relationship with your family and your home routine. It's like a spaceship coming back to earth and the astronauts having to adjust to an entirely different atmosphere. And just like a spaceship's bumpy ride as it re-enters the atmosphere skipping along, it can be a bit bumpy at home until you find your familiar tempo.

What advice would you give to artists about health and wellness while touring?
Pace yourself. The road is tough. If you are pouring it on every day and night, you are going to hit the wall. When touring, you are playing the long game. You need to perform to the best of your abilities at every show in every city. You also have to give good, well-thought-out interviews. The artists who have career longevity, who have remained touring for over forty years, are the ones with a work ethic. Yes, there can be some partying here and there, but these artists are staying in shape, eating healthy, and even working out while on the road. David Gilmour from Pink Floyd once told me, "People think we just sit around, get high, and play. Nothing could be further from the truth. I go to the office every day with my guitar the same way you go to your office everyday with your briefcase. I know what Pink Floyd is, and it's my job to be the best Pink Floyd possible. We all work very hard at that."

Younger artists may just see the glitz and party side of the music business. If you really want to make it, have fun once in a while, but keep your eye on the ball. Push yourself toward excellence. Ask yourself how you can continually make your show better. How you can entertain an audience so well that you guarantee yourself a standing ovation and an encore. That's a job. A lot of musicians think it's just a lifestyle, but it's a real job, and you need to stay healthy to complete your mission.

Whatever managers, agents, press, or promotion people you are working with, ask them for reasonable interview schedules and build in a lunch every day for yourself. Even if it's only light fare, you need a rest stop to catch your breath and recharge your batteries for the rest of the day and for your performance that evening.

Do you, or did you carry a bag of essentials on the road with you?
Yes! And still do to this day. I have a few very nice-looking crossbody bags and leather shoulder bags as well. It's an old habit from being on the road for so many years with artists. I always have my wallet, sunglasses, extra contact lenses, contact saline solution, Pepto-Bismol, Advil, sunscreen, Neosporin, Band-aids, emery board, hand cream, a small aerosol spray of cologne, and sometimes even a small deodorant. Just things that make life easier for you, in case you need them when you're out and about.

You'd be surprised how many people ask to use the stuff I carry. If I take out my hand cream, everybody wants some. Band-Aids or sunscreen always come in handy, and I can't tell you how many men and women have asked me if I have any Advil or Tylenol!

When you're on a tour you always have to be prepared. In the middle of the night when there's nobody to turn to, you need to be your own doctor. If your stomach is upset from too much rock and roll lifestyle, Pepto-Bismol will save you. If you lose a contact lens at a concert, better have another and the solution to put it in. If you're working all day, don't have time to return to your hotel, and want to freshen up before dinner and a night out, it's great having that small deodorant and some cologne. You can wash up in any restroom, re-apply, and voila, you're ready for part two.

When working with artists in different situations these items can come in very handy, indeed. I had to put Band-Aids on the hands of both Johnny Cash and Tony Bennett on separate occasions when, somehow, they'd cut themselves. Cash in the recording studio, and Tony on the set of a television show I was producing. On each occasion no one could find a first aid kit and there I was, Johnny-on-the-spot. I can tell you they really appreciated my road bag then because they were able to carry on with their work without missing a beat. As I was putting the Band-Aid on Cash's hand, I remember thinking, "Wow, that's the hand that's played all those famous chords!"

STRESS

CHAPTER 4

THE EFFECTS OF STRESS

Suggested Listening: "Sleep On Needles"
— S O N D R E   L E R C H E

There are a few different types of stress. There is "good" stress (also called "eustress") and "bad" stress. A few examples of eustress might be things like that rush that helps you push through a race, getting an exciting promotion at work, or the endorphin high we feel after a great date. Hormones such as adrenaline, oxytocin, serotonin, and endorphins are released, but not cortisol, the stress hormone that has been linked to adverse health effects like depression, sleep disturbance, weight gain, and digestive issues, to name a few.

However, when we experience negative stress for more than a few minutes (for example, feeling overwhelmed or uncertain over current events, experiencing difficulties in relationships, or worrying about someone's health), we get a rush of adrenaline, cortisol, and norepinephrine to help push through and deal with what our body perceives as a threat. When that negative stress is chronic, so is the release of cortisol.

The nervous system is greatly affected by stress. When exposed to stress, the sympathetic nervous system (SNS) goes into "fight or flight" mode, shifting the body's resources toward allowing you to fight off an enemy or predator—or run the hell away from it.

When this happens, the SNS signals the adrenal glands, which sit on top of the kidneys, to secrete adrenalin (aka epinephrine) and cortisol. This causes the heart rate to increase as well as blood pressure, and for glucose levels to rise in response to the perceived emergency your body is preparing to deal with. Overstimulation of the parasympathetic nervous system (PNS) can also have profound effects on our stress response.

When you "freeze," your body is preparing to fight or flee. Similar physiological changes are happening, but you are completely still, preparing for the next move. Like the fight and flight response, freezing is also involuntary.

You've likely experienced for yourself a range of physical, mental, emotional, and behavioral effects of stress at one time or another. Let's explore some of the most common ones.

Physical Effects of Stress

Stress can impact our physical health in numerous ways. All of our body systems could potentially be impacted. Here are some of the most common physical manifestations of stress[1]:

- musculoskeletal pain (ex: tension headaches, back and neck pain);
- increase in production of steroid hormones called glucocorticoids (cortisol is one example), which can lead to elevated blood glucose levels;
- gastrointestinal distress such as gas, bloating, diarrhea, and general discomfort;
- flare-ups of existing digestive disorders such as Irritable Bowel Syndrome, Crohn's, or Colitis;
- heartburn or acid reflux;

- sleep problems;
- impaired immune system function;
- infertility;
- miscarriage;
- amenorrhea or changes in menstrual cycle;
- worsening of menopausal symptoms;
- increased heart rate;
- inflammation in the circulatory system, especially in the coronary arteries;
- heart disease;
- high blood pressure;
- increased cholesterol levels;
- low libido;
- nausea and vomiting;
- overstimulation of the adrenal glands,
- shortness of breath;
- stomach ulcers; and
- asthma attacks (in cases of extreme stress).

Mental Effects of Stress

Stress can take a significant toll on our mental and emotional health.[2]

For example, chronic stress has been associated with:

- increased anxiety;
- depression;
- sadness;
- irritability or anger;
- lack of focus;
- feeling overwhelmed; and
- lack of motivation.

Behavioral Effects of Stress

Our behaviors can also become greatly impacted by stress. Some very common ways in which this can happen may include:

- changes in eating (ex. undereating or overeating);
- changes in exercise (ex. exercising less or exercising too much);
- social withdrawal;
- angry or emotional outbursts;
- drug or alcohol abuse or misuse; and
- smoking.

Throughout the course of my dad's illness, I certainly experienced a number of these. While I was eating well and exercising, I was not sleeping well at all. The second I would turn the lights off, I would get a jolt of energy. I finally just started sleeping with the lights on. Reading fiction has long been a nighttime ritual of mine, but in those first few months, it seemed that every single book I picked up had a character with pancreatic cancer or a dead dad somewhere in the backstory. Why couldn't authors come up with another way to kill off their protagonist's parents and partners? There are over a hundred different types of cancer alone—was the pancreas really that much more literary than other organs?

If CBD had been more widely available, I would have certainly explored that as a sleep aid. Benadryl helped sometimes, but then I'd be groggy the next morning, so I tried to keep that to a minimum.

Because of the sleep deprivation and stress, my immune system took a serious hit. My wake-up call came when an infection from a manicure took almost six months to heal, complete with multiple rounds of antibiotics (during which I learned the hard way that I'm allergic to sulfa drugs—whoops). Because the antibiotics destroyed all the good bacteria in my system too, I found myself feeling foggy-headed and developed some new food sensitivities—hallmark signs of gut health issues. During this time, I was still counseling patients and generating content intended to help people heal themselves and feel well, but behind the scenes, I felt like I was falling apart.

CHAPTER 5

HOW TO BREAK THE STRESS CYCLE

Suggested Listening: "A Shot in The Arm"

—WILCO

C hronic stress is an easy cycle to get caught up in. When we're in the midst of it, it can feel impossible to see a way out. We may become overwhelmed when we think all the stressors we face. If you're physically and emotionally exhausted from taking a loved one to lots of doctors' appointments, for example, it can be tough to think clearly or strategically about what you can do to feel more rested.

It always makes my heart hurt when someone tells me they were told they should reduce their stress but then received zero guidance on how to do so. That well-intentioned but lackluster recommendation also misses the big distinction between a stressor and our stress response. There are always going to be external stressors we can't really do anything about, but what we *can* control is how we respond to those stressors. And good news: It doesn't have to be complicated. In fact, simple is often most effective.

Rather than trying to fix the big stuff, focus on breaking the stress cycle. Remove the pressure to eliminate stress and instead make it about disrupting the pattern at an approachable point.

Step One: Identify What You Can and Cannot Control

It can feel like a bummer to think about what's out of our hands, so practice reframing those thoughts to be about what you *can* do. For example, if you're stressed out about feeling like you have no time for yourself because you're juggling so many things, maybe you can start to protect your time and energy by saying "no" to things that aren't truly essential or having a conversation with your employer about your workload.

Step Two: Notice Where You Struggle

Without judgment, observe how this stress may be impacting your physical, mental, or behavioral health. Maybe having to take a loved one to appointments prevents you from going to the workout class that used to be a regular part of your routine, and you've since fallen way out of the habit with exercise. You want to be more active again because you know it would help you have better energy and make you feel healthier overall, but you're feeling stuck. Or maybe you're having a hard time eating well because you're short on time to shop, plan, and cook healthy meals. Once you know what the problem is, you can start exploring the root causes and taking stock of what you may be able to do something about.

Step Three: Pick a Tool to Start With

Make your stress management approach about habits that fit sustainably into your existing lifestyle and don't be afraid to start small. Going with the exercise example above, maybe try getting up thirty minutes earlier a few days a week to do an at-home workout. Or maybe doing fifteen minutes of physical activity in the morning and fifteen minutes when you get home at night would work better for you. And if multiple days a week feels like too much to start with, try one day a week and gradually increase as you feel ready.

Step Four: Be Flexible

It's okay for our stress management plans to change as our needs, schedules, and priorities shift over time. Check in with yourself regularly about what's working and what's not. It can also help to have a few versions of your plans. Maybe there's a weekday and a weekend version, or a version for weeks you're feeling extra stressed, and a plan for weeks where you feel you have it more together or don't need to be as intentional about carving out time for self-care.

Step Five: Get Support

There's no shame in asking for help. In fact, it's a sign of strength. No one of us is built to do every single thing ourselves. Often, when we have a lot on our plate and are taking care of others, it's easy to get sucked into the limiting belief that our needs don't matter as much as the needs of others. Again, this is an area where you can start small if the idea of asking for and accepting support is a lot. Come up with something specific that you need help with.

CHAPTER 6

THE ALIEN

Suggested Listening: "Space Oddity"
—DAVID BOWIE

M ostly I just kept telling myself that this situation was tempo- rary and that I just had to push through. Because, gener- ally speaking, the prognosis for pancreatic cancer is so poor, we really didn't know how much time we had left with my dad (Weeks? Months? A year?), but we knew it was limited. At the oncologist's urging, my sister moved up her wedding from May to September—barely three months away—so we were thrown into wedding planning.

The day my dad first met with his team, while my parents spent the afternoon in appointments, my sister, her best friend Melina (aka my bonus sister), and I went wedding dress shopping down- town. We drank champagne and tried to focus on bridal stuff, but it was hard to ignore that my mother was missing—and why.

I remember sitting in the dressing room looking at my calendar on my phone, wondering how long or short of a road this might be and wishing desperately that someone could just tell me what to plan for. What would I need? And if I quit any of my jobs, would I make enough money? What could I let go of? Who should I contact to drum up freelance work? I also had to write a great sister of the bride speech. I specifically tried not to think about how there was basically no chance my dad would be at my own wedding.

My dad's cancer was noted to be "unstageable" because, like many sneaky GI cancers, it had spread. There were lesions in his liver, kidneys, the outside lining of the stomach, and the lungs as well. Because of its location at the bottom of the pancreas, the primary tumor was deemed inoperable, so chemotherapy, including an experimental trial drug, was recommended. A port was placed at the same time the biopsy was done so the doctors could learn more about the cancer cells.

The team offered us the chance to look at the operating room before the procedure. I found the OR environment oddly soothing—I find it comforting to understand how things work so was grateful for the opportunity to demystify the procedure. It was so quiet in there you would have had no idea that New York City was the beyond the walls.

A little while later, when he'd been wheeled out to Recovery and we found the Mets game for him on TV, he was in good spirits. When we got my sister on the phone, the first thing he said to her was a playful "My new boobs look amazing!" I waited around until my mom told me to just go home and get some rest.

When I got back to my building on the Upper West Side that night, there were police cars and tape out front. When I finally got into the lobby, the doorman told me that a man had tried to jump. I'd just come from my dad's bedside where he'd talked about how badly he wanted to live—that's some damn awful irony. I felt numb as I packed my suitcase to get ready for the next day's trip to New Jersey.

My dad had a few days before treatment started where he felt well enough to go out, so I joined my parents for dinner out the next night. Some of my dad's friends were there, and I watched him laughing and joking with them even as he filled them in on what was going on. He unbuttoned the top buttons of his shirt to show them his port, aka "The Alien."

When my dad started chemo, it became very clear very fast that I needed to step up and be there more. The side effects of the experimental drug were outlined in a thick binder, and he experienced *lots* of them. An entire shelf in the kitchen was now devoted to medications. My mom would text me pictures of his labs and ask questions about his symptoms and care.

I got a few of my shifts covered at the hospital so I could catch my breath and figure out what to do next. It was clear that working seven days a week just wasn't going to fly anymore. I knew that I was going to have to let go of that clinical job, which was per diem (hourly, with no vacation or sick days or benefits). Besides the unpredictable schedule, I also suddenly found myself unable to focus on patient care as normal.

One morning I even did something I'd sworn I'd never do: I cried in a patient's room. They were going on about the food quality and demanding I go down into the kitchen to make them something else, and I just started weeping. What I was really upset about, of course, was that my father would never live to be as old as this patient. Thank goodness one of the diet techs (who had way more control over the food and *could* fix the problem) just happened to be walking by and swooped in to save me.

I retreated to the nurses' station and a weekend nurse I'd never met before came up and enveloped me in a bear hug. I wasn't much of a hugger or crier, but in plain view of anyone who happened to be walking by, I sobbed into a stranger's chest. I choked out that my dad was sick and that I didn't know if I could be good at this job anymore. I was so embarrassed, but she made me feel like it was okay to be a human, even when in uniform.

I gave my two weeks' notice the next day. My supervisor and I talked about my taking a leave of absence for a few months, but deep down, I knew I wouldn't be ready to go back by then. I took my little emergency poetry notebook, favorite pen, and deodorant out of my lab coat pockets and made sure the pager was switched off.

It was so unceremonious. I'd always imagined quitting my per diem job because I'd landed some incredible full-time opportunity or had too many private clients or was so busy with writing or teaching or speaking that I needed to make space. Instead, I just told my manager, "My dad has inoperable cancer and we don't know how long he has, and I need to be there. It's kind of that simple."

While my mom was the primary caregiver for my dad, my sister and I helped out with running errands, taking him to appointments, preparing food, making sure he got the right meds at the right time, and also just hanging out with him. I can't speak for my sister, but I felt like I was making up for all those years when I had put my career above everything—and everyone—else in my life.

At least I could do virtual coaching and I could write and do content creation projects from my parents' house, from the chemo suite and the hospital waiting room, even from the NJ Transit bus if need be. My goal was to just make up the lost income from that hospital job and stay afloat through my dad's cancer treatment. I'd worry about business growth and sustainability later. I would miss being part of a healthcare team and the clinical routine I had come to take comfort and pride in, but I knew it was the right thing for my family. I also knew I was fortunate to be able to make a big change like that. On the outside (and on social media) I was telling a story about staking out on an entrepreneurial journey, but behind the scenes, it was obviously a different story, one that my family chose not to share publicly.

My mom, sister, and I were all in "helping" professions. They're psychotherapists, and I'm a dietitian and health coach. Because we were responsible for others' well-being outside of our family, we each had to find our own ways with setting boundaries and implementing the appropriate self-care—as best we could, anyway. My mom chose to tell her existing clients what was going on, but she did refer new clients out during my dad's illness. My sister, on the other hand, opted not to share with clients. For the most part, I kept quiet about it, though as his illness progressed, I did share with a few people in my real life who needed to know for logistical reasons.

We all had our reality-check moments. I'll share mine in another chapter, but my mom developed Bell's palsy. She had had it on the other side of her face, right after my parents got married, and a few weeks after my sister's wedding, she woke up with one side of her face drooping. "As well as I was doing," she says, "it made me realize, well, maybe not." She started seeing her own therapist weekly, worked from home when she could, and went for regular walks. "Even though I couldn't stop working, I did spend more time with your dad because we both knew he wasn't going to be around forever."

CHAPTER 7

WATCH OUT FOR CAREGIVER BURNOUT

Suggested Listening: "I Need Never Get Old"
—NATHANIEL RATELIFF & THE NIGHT SWEATS

"Caregiver burnout" is a term used to describe the physical, mental, and emotional exhaustion a caregiver may face, and it can happen when caregivers don't get the care and support they need, or if they try to do more than they are physically or financially capable of. Stressed out caregivers may also experience anxiety, depression, or fatigue—sometimes all three. Caregiver burnout may be accompanied by shifts in attitude toward the person to whom you are giving care. For example, you may notice your thoughts go from positive and nurturing to feelings of resentment or other negative thoughts. It's also very common for caregivers to feel guilty about spending time, money, or energy on themselves rather than on the person they're taking care of.[3]

Some of the most common contributing factors of caregiver burnout are unrealistic expectations and unreasonable demands (especially of themselves), lack of control, and role confusion where they have been a parent, partner, spouse, child, sibling, or friend, and find themselves suddenly pushed into the caregiver role and have a hard time adjusting. There are other factors that can come up as well. For example, if someone has a lot of demands on them, professionally or financially, like if they work for themselves and don't have paid vacation time or if they need to keep working because their partner is medically unable to work, it can add extra stress to their life.

Signs that you may be struggling with caregiver burnout may include:

- changes in appetite or eating patterns;
- changes in weight;
- changes in sleep;
- emotional and/or physical exhaustion;
- feeling "down" or in some cases, feelings of hopelessness;
- impaired immune system function;
- irritability;
- loss of interest in activities you used to enjoy;
- thoughts of wanting to hurt yourself or the person you're caring for; and
- withdrawal from friends, family, and colleagues.

One of the most important steps for dealing with caregiver burnout is to acknowledge it and to give yourself permission to seek support. Release the shame or guilt you may feel.

Lauren Fasanella is a licensed clinical social worker who has worked extensively in the hospital setting, assisting patients and their families with coordinating and managing care. By this point, she says, "I can just look at a person and tell a lot by the way they look. If the caregiver doesn't look robust and healthy, if they look unkempt, that's a sign to me that it's burnout."

A big part of this, she explains, is because they're so focused on their caregiving duties, they barely think of their own care.

"That could be from day-to-day things like not eating properly, hydrating, or sleeping, to bigger things like missing their annual dental exam or primary care physician check-up. They do that because they don't want to leave the person or are so overwhelmed with caretaking, they don't even think of their own needs."

Financial burdens are also a concern for caregivers, Fasanella points out. "If they're financially strapped, that can trickle down to affect health and self-care. Or they may struggle if they can only afford to have someone care for the person while they're at work and then when they're off, they're the caregiver and get no downtime to recharge."

In addition to mood changes, irritability, and feeling down, another sign that someone may be on the road to caregiver burnout is a tendency toward extremes. For example, she says, "They're hyperfocused on the details and have taken the caregiving to an extreme. When they are scrutinizing the little things, you know they have taken it on as part of their identity and every aspect of it, and they are not getting enough in their own life. You want to be thorough—you don't want to make medication errors—but when they are hyperfocusing on things that are not as important, that's a sign that they're struggling."

Getting Started with Finding Support for Caregiver Burnout

If you're afraid of asking for help, Fasanella recommends, "Put yourself in their shoes. What would you say or how would you feel if a friend or family member feeling overwhelmed came to you and said, 'I need help.' Would you say no? Wouldn't you be happy to help that person if you were in a position to help them?"

For her patients' families and clients who are caregivers, she tries to normalize asking for help and reminds them that if they're burned out, they can't be the caregiver they want to be. She also thinks it's important to acknowledge that control plays a role.

When you are in a situation where there may be a lot of things beyond your control (such as when a loved one has a serious illness), it is very normal and human to find yourself clinging to what you *can* control. However, that desire to control can quickly set you on the path to burnout. "When we become a caregiver, there is a level of control that people can become fixated on, and it becomes difficult to relinquish that control. You need support in that relinquishing."

There are different ways to seek and accept that support.

Make a list of what you need help with. It can be big things or little things. Feeling stumped? Fasanella recommends asking yourself what it would be helpful to have someone come in and do with you or for you.

Take small steps. If you are freaking out over the idea of releasing some control, it's okay to start with just one small thing to give yourself a chance to see how it feels to have a little more breathing room.

Start with your network. Knowing the people from whom you are accepting help may feel more approachable than hiring a stranger. However, others may have the opposite experience and may feel comfortable if someone they have no familial or social ties to, as that may cut out feelings of obligation to return the favor.

Ask your doctor's office to see if they have any disease-specific agencies they can recommend locally or nationally. They may also have a social worker or nurse who could tell you where to start in preventing and managing burnout.

Understand your insurance benefits. This is a big one Fasanella highlights. "A lot of times clients and patients don't understand what their benefits are: employer-based, medical. Call your insurance company to see what's available to you. Call your employer or HR to find out what caregiver support may be available. For example, is there family leave? Is it paid or unpaid? These are all resources to look into."

Take veteran status into account. "The other resource I think people may not be aware of," says Fasanella, "is if someone is a veteran and has many resources available to them. If the patient is a veteran, I recommend they go to their local VA office and meet with a social worker. They also have tremendous resources for caregivers of veterans. So many veterans don't realize they are eligible for services, and they are so plentiful."

Explore the internet for resources. While it can be overwhelming, a Google search is another way to seek and find support you can benefit from. "If you're not tech savvy," Fasanella adds, "have a friend or family member do that for you. That's another way of asking for help."

Consider a support group, if it will serve you.

CHAPTER 8

DON'T IGNORE
WARNING SIGNS

Suggested Listening: "Marie Provost"
—NICK LOWE

When we're caught up in worrying about others in our life, it's easy not to notice warning signals the body sends about our own health, or to put off routine screenings because we feel we can't or shouldn't take that time.

Because one of my biggest self-care struggles was sleep, I experienced a sharp decline in my immune system function. I was used to bouncing back from pretty much anything very quickly, so I was shocked when an infection from a manicure knocked me on my ass. I ended up with a chronic paronychia (an infection around the nails typically caused by bacteria and/or yeast) that hung out for months under my left thumbnail.

Despite using home remedies, it persisted, so I tried oral antibiotics. The first two rounds did nothing, and the infection got worse. Drilling a small hole in the nail didn't get all the pus out, so finally it just had to be removed. In the meantime, I was placed on another type of antibiotic I'd never tried before. I didn't think I was allergic to any drugs, so when the telltale rash began to spread, I wrote it off as an eczema outbreak, something I'd experienced at various times in my life. It certainly seemed logical, given the amount of stress I was under and the fact that it was February. I even went to an urgent care clinic the night I took off my pants and saw that I'd broken out all over my legs and feet and was sent home with a prescription for high-strength hydrocortisone cream.

When I got up for work the next morning after a rough night of half-sleep, I was so uncomfortable, I didn't even want to put clothes on.

"You can't call in sick because you don't want to wear pants," I told myself. "Totally unprofessional."

I think on some level, I knew something was up. My throat had started to get itchy, which scared me. By some small miracle, it happened to be my day at my corporate wellness job in an employee wellness center where there were multiple nurses on staff. The hope that they'd know what to do motivated me to get it together and get out the door that morning.

As soon as I walked in, they took a look at my face, which had started to redden, and at my eyes, which were slowly starting to swell shut, and asked, "Are you . . . okay?" They knew about the saga of my left thumb, so when I explained my symptoms, they knew right away what was happening.

I was past the point of using an EpiPen and going to the ER, they explained. "So we're going to give you Benadryl, stat. Then we're going to cancel all your patients and you're going to lie in the back room so we can keep an eye on you."

Thankfully, I responded well. I must have needed the Benadryl so badly I didn't even feel high—though my email history from that day tells a different story. I didn't tell my parents until much later in the day what had happened because I didn't want to worry them, though I did reach out to a few friends in case I needed someone to come check on me to make sure I was still alive. I was sent home on a standard course of steroids and (more) Benadryl to get me through the week as the drug worked its way out of my system.

I was still living alone at the time, and I remember waking up in the middle of the night with my feet itching. It was terrifying—the idea that if I'd tried to sleep it off that morning, my throat would have started to close and maybe I wouldn't have made it to the phone in time. The kind of death every single New York City girl dreads, where no one knows you've died until the smell drifts into the hall, but not before your pets eat your face.

Anyway, I guess I'm sharing this to show you that, yes, I'm a licensed healthcare professional, but at times I have been checked out of my own health. I was so distracted by what was going on with my dad, I brushed off major warning signals, despite telling my patients to take their own health seriously.

Though the example I shared above was related to physical health, this could also pertain to mental and emotional health as well as to financial health. If something is starting to seem off or you feel like you're losing your handle on an aspect of your wellness, please don't be afraid to seek support. It's easier to address a concern when it's something small than when it's a full-blown emergency. Yes, you may worry about concerning a loved one who depends on you, but you will feel much better knowing that you addressed a problem before it got out of hand and affected them in an irreversible way.

CHAPTER 9

FIX WHAT YOU CAN

Suggested Listening: "Changes"
—LANGHORNE SLIM & THE LAW

One of the key parts of stress management is acknowledging what you can and cannot control and then start with taking steps to address what is within your reach.

When it comes to caregiver burnout, it can be so easy to brush our own needs aside and for some, to even wear our burnout like a badge of honor—in some ways, it's not that far off from the hustle culture that leads so many entrepreneurs to drive themselves into the ground. Or the grueling rehearsal, performance, and interview schedule that wears a musician or actor out. For better and worse, there's no reward given for the caregiver who suffers the most, and trading in our own health and well-being won't magically result in our loved one recovering from their illness.

Fix what you can. It may not prevent you from moments of feeling paralyzed by fear and worry around things that are beyond your control, but aside from helping you feel better, physically, the sense of accomplishment that comes from overcoming a self-care challenge can trickle into other areas of your life and help you feel more resilient.

Let's use nutrition as an example.

Changes in eating habits comes up for many caregivers. This can be for a wide variety of reasons, but some of the most common ones are changes to their schedule, having less time to shop for and prepare food, stress-related food cravings, and emotional eating. This often results in higher intake of convenience foods, fast foods, sugar, and junk food, and with that, weight gain, changes in lab values (like glucose or cholesterol, for example), decreased energy, poor mood, and changes in cognitive function. When you compound that with increased levels of stress hormones like cortisol and adrenaline thanks to physical or emotional stress, lack of sleep, and / or having increased demands on their time, it's not hard to see why caregivers are so at risk for poor health outcomes themselves.

I can understand that overhauling your diet and going all-in on healthy eating may be the last thing you'd want to do when you already feel stretched—and the good news is that you don't have to make sweeping changes. I'll share more about this in the nutrition section, but for a little taste, let's focus for a moment on how eating for blood sugar balance can help you feel more stable and less susceptible to being caught off guard by energy crashes.

Making sure we include protein, fat, and fiber in our meals and snacks can help buffer the breakdown of carbohydrates we eat and lead to a much smaller arc and dip—and more stable blood sugar. Aside from supporting more stable energy, this can also help you feel more satisfied and less likely to struggle with compulsive snacking. It also happens to be beneficial for our body's stress response.

So if one thing you are not able to do anything about is having a lack of time to prepare food, something you *can* do is make more mindful choices when you're buying food outside the home or ordering takeout, keeping an eye toward having a balance of protein, fat, and carbs and incorporating fiber-rich vegetables, fruit, and whole grains. Here are a few examples of first-step solutions that have worked for my clients and patients:

- If you'd normally grab a donut, try scrambled egg on whole grain toast or an English muffin.
- Add veggies to an omelet.
- Instead of a sugary yogurt parfait, have plain Greek yogurt and a banana or other fruit.
- Instead of ordering a burrito with rice and beans inside, try black beans, fajita veggies, and guacamole and piling on salsa.
- Instead of two slices of pizza, have one slice of pizza and a side salad.
- When having a sandwich, swap in whole grain bread and have a side salad instead of chips.
- Instead of breaded and fried chicken, go for grilled or baked.

These are just some ideas to get the wheels turning. Why these have been successful for my patients and clients (and myself) is that they don't require major changes—just tweaking your order slightly instead of trying to dive into cooking from scratch or finding new places to eat, which can be stressful when you already feel like you have no time and want to stick to what you know and what is easy.

Another positive: the examples above are more balanced and will support more stable blood sugar, which can improve energy, mood, and resilience. Seeing how much better you feel with small changes can be motivating to continue with making realistic lifestyle changes that support your goals and help you feel well as time goes on.

If nothing else, making it more convenient to eat healthfully can give you a mental boost of, "Cool, I can at least do that."

If you're used to worrying about the big stuff and making sure others are okay, thinking about your own needs can take some getting used to—massive understatement, I know. If you need to, take it in small doses. If you don't feel ready to take on a bigger struggle you're having, start with a small issue.

INTERVIEW WITH
JOHN MELLENCAMP

Suggested Listening: "Pink Houses"
—JOHN MELLENCAMP

J ohn Mellencamp is an American musician, singer-songwriter, Farm Aid cofounder, actor, director, and painter. He and my dad worked together for the better part of thirty years. I have a few memories of hanging out in the bowels of venues like Jones Beach while my dad touched base with him before a show. I mostly remember that they teased each other a lot about getting old, which is funny to think of now, given how young they actually were then.

The first time I ever interviewed Mr. Mellencamp was in 2007 for the entertainment section of a free Boston magazine that no longer exists when he was coming to town for a show. I doubt he remembers that conversation, but it went off on a memorable (for me) tangent about polyploidy strawberries. Almost fifteen years later he was kind enough to make time to speak with me for this book about his experience as a touring musician.

What are some of the physical health challenges of touring?
I've toured for so long, for forty years, and it has changed

dramatically for me. In the seventies it was a gang of guys on a bus—today it's something totally different. As a young person, I never worried about my health. When you're twenty-one years old, you're bulletproof. I had a heart attack when I was forty-two. Up until then, there are no exercise routines, just do the shows, hang around, more of that old adage of the rock and roll lifestyle, but then everything changed. I started eating better. I have my own meals prepared for me now. I didn't back then. Me touring now is basically, I go from my dressing room (which is an Airstream that comes all over the country with me) to the stage, do my show, walk back to the Airstream, get in the car, and leave.

What are some of the mental and emotional challenges?

People have the total wrong idea of what touring is about. I don't know how many times people will walk up to me and say, "Boy, you really had fun onstage." I was *working*. It's my job. I've been to a million amazing places but I haven't gotten to see them because I had work to do.

Yeah, you get stage fright, exhaustion, getting so worn out you're negative all the time. When asking about mental stress, what you're asking is why is the sky blue. There's a billion reasons. You can't put your finger on one thing and say this is what's stressful.

What advice would you give to artists about health and wellness while touring? Or is there anything you wish you had known when you were just starting out?

It's hard to answer that question because the music business has changed so dramatically, but I guess it would be, "Are you sure you want to do this?" This is nothing like people think it is.

What is something that would surprise most people or that people get wrong about life on the road?

People have the illusion from the way rock and roll started in the fifties that it's a party, but it's my job to entertain people, to make sure they have a good time, hopefully have a shared experience. You can't do that high or on drugs. Nobody wants to see somebody stumbling onstage drunk. I think my message is, whatever you think being on tour is about, you're wrong. The only thing that's not wrong is the shared experience onstage.

When you're on the road, do you carry a bag of essentials? If so, what's in there?

I've never had any trouble with my voice, ever. The only thing I make sure I have is baking soda because sometimes you end up eating food on the road that will give you heartburn, and baking soda with Perrier can help with that. I take a spoonful of baking soda in half a bottle of Perrier a half hour before I go onstage. It's a remedy my grandfather taught me many years ago. I also never eat before I go on.

NUTRITION

CHAPTER 10

SUGAR FIEND

Suggested Listening: "I Won't Back Down"
—JOHNNY CASH

"Chicken Cordon Bleus (Live)"
—STEVE GOODMAN

M y dad didn't want us sharing anything about his illness on social media, but in real life, it was something we could talk about on a need-to-know basis. Inevitably, when my dad's cancer came up, the first thing anyone would say to me was, "Your dad is so lucky to have a dietitian for a daughter."

I would just do the smile-and-nod. The truth of it was that my dad didn't want me to be his dietitian; he wanted me to be his daughter. In fact, he would get pissed if I ever went as far as making a suggestion of something he should eat that might alleviate a side effect or symptom he was having or give him more energy. We had a family rule that had been established many years before: Jess is not allowed to tell Dad what to eat. I had wondered initially if a cancer diagnosis would inspire my dad to change his habits, but if anything, it had made him even more stubborn about not wanting to be told what to do.

He could ask me for advice (which he did occasionally), but I was *not* allowed to offer it. Sometimes I went behind his back and talked to my mom about some things to try, though. For example, when he had muscle cramps—a side effect of the first trial drug—here were some foods with high potassium to feed him (I remember a Rice Krispies-with-banana phase, for example). When he developed a cough and terrible mouth sores, we got very creative with milkshakes. We'd look at his labs together and try to figure out what we needed to pay attention to. Not everything could be addressed with diet, but a lot could.

Deep down, I carried a lot of shame. Here I was, a licensed professional who knew a lot about nutrition and lifestyle factors and cancer risk reduction, and I hadn't been able to "save" my own dad. That was ignoring the deeper hurt, though: he didn't want my help. My dad was an emotional guy, and my entire life, I'd watched him gravitate toward sugar, red meat, and junk food. If he was ever going to change, it was going to be on his terms. He had always been active and would go through phases where he was more focused on eating healthfully, but it rarely stuck.

I knew it wasn't my job to save him and that it wasn't about me, but I felt responsible. In my bad moments, I would think about all the ways I'd failed to foster an environment where he felt inspired and empowered to change for himself.

After a cancer diagnosis, some people overhaul their habits. They clean up their diets, lace up their sneakers, and then they go forth and preach the gospel of good health. Some do this thoughtfully and effectively, taking an inclusive approach to cultivating community and inspiring others. On the flip side, there are some who can come off as being overly militant or judgmental. I get upset by the patient-shaming and fearmongering that goes on—so much pressure to identify the bad habit that caused someone's cancer. There's also tons of misinformation out there. While we do have a lot of data on modifiable risk factors and diet and lifestyle approaches to reduce risk or improve treatment experience, there's also a lot of garbage to sift through, and it's not always easy to tell what's credible and what's not.

My dad had zero interest in signing up for the lifestyle change approach, and it was important to me that he feel loved and supported, so I focused on showing up where he needed me to meet him. If that meant watching him live on donuts and ice cream for weeks at a time because that was what would go down and stay down? Fine. With colleagues, I tried to keep nutrition-related conversations about my dad to a minimum. Not only had I not prevented his cancer, but I was also not pestering him to eat vegetables or stop eating red meat. He knew he was free to ask me questions, which he sometimes did, but he certainly wasn't asking me to make him spiced lentils or mushroom broth.

For better and worse, the chemo made it easier to let go of my ego with the food stuff. There were times he could barely keep anything down and had virtually no appetite. One of the drugs caused such severe cramps in his hands he could barely hold a fork. Those weeks and months were really about survival and just getting calories into him. He had minimal desire to eat, anyway. Sometimes he would finally feel a hint of an appetite for some specific food, but by the time we'd made or bought it for him, the moment had passed and he was too wiped out to have more than a few bites.

Not surprisingly, the only thing that helped him was marijuana. While it hadn't been a part of his life before cancer, it became a useful tool for him. The moment the nurse practitioner on his team said, "While we can't legally prescribe it, we can strongly encourage it" was a huge relief. Though his oncologist was in New York State (where medicinal marijuana wasn't yet an option), as a New Jersey resident, he was able to get a prescription.

I will never forget the summer afternoon we got a family tutorial in how to pack a bowl for him. He immediately took a huge hit, and then went and sat in the other room. About fifteen minutes later my mom and I went in to check on him. He had his hoodie up over his head and was staring at the dark TV.

"How are you doing, Jim?"

"We're going out."

"Where are we going?"

"Guess."

My mom listed off a few of his usual places.

He shook his head. "We're going to White Castle."

So the four of us jumped in the car and drove to the nearest White Castle. As I sat in the back seat with my bottled water and watched him house three burgers and a shake, I took a mental snapshot of the moment. I remember thinking I should probably be grossed out, but I was honestly just relieved—and a bit amused.

Once he got a handle on what the right dosage and form of cannabis was best for him (he learned quickly that a vape pen cartridge should last longer than, like, a day), if you didn't know he was using it, you likely wouldn't have noticed at all—to my mind, the fact that he didn't seem high said a lot about how much discomfort he was in and how much he needed that relief just to function.

One of the things that helped me tremendously when I felt myself starting to get stressed out by my dad's food choices was to come back to the things we connected on. For us, that was music. We would send each other songs and videos by our favorite artists (like the recording I found of Elvis Costello and T Bone Burnett singing "Ring of Fire" together) or other great covers of old favorites we came across (The Milk Carton Kids' recording of Pink Floyd's "Wish You Were Here" floored us both, and we loved Johnny Cash singing Tom Petty's "I Won't Back Down") and on days he felt well, I would ask him questions about his years working in the music business.

Of course, I loved hearing the behind-the-scenes stuff, but I was also interested in learning about his career path and hearing any wisdom he had to share. Because I was flying solo with no clear roadmap, and also because I suddenly found myself frequently being tapped for interviews and seeing my name in national news outlets, I craved career advice. Though our industries were so different, as I got deeper into the media side of wellness to supplement my income, I saw there were some similarities when you looked below the surface.

We talked sometimes about recording a podcast together where we would play songs and he would tell stories about their creation or the artists behind them, but he had a terrible cough from the medication (and sure, probably all the cancer that had traveled to his lungs) and even after it went away, he was just too tired most of the time. For years he had talked casually about writing a book, but after his diagnosis, we never brought it up.

Looking back, I also wonder if on some level my dad just didn't want to spill any dirt. While he had an "I don't care what anyone thinks" way about him, when it came to his work and especially his artists, he was very respectful and guarded about their privacy. I can count on one hand the number of musicians I'd heard him speak poorly about, and even that was in our home with just our immediate family there. I often thought of my dad's closed-lip approach when I was working at major hospitals in NYC and friends would ask for details about celebrity patients. I'd usually just change the subject or say there was really nothing that exciting to tell—just another day at work.

CHAPTER 11

A SMALL COLLECTION OF UNSOLICITED ADVICE AND UNHELPFUL COMMENTS

Suggested Listening: "Sisters of Mercy"
—LEONARD COHEN

"Handle With Care"
—JENNY LEWIS AND THE WATSON TWINS

"When my dad had cancer he went plant-based and now he's super-healthy."

"Have you tried juicing?"

"Maybe if your dad had been using this juice-based supplement he wouldn't have gotten cancer in the first place."

"Does your dad eat a lot of meat? I have this great vegan cookbook I can loan you."

"Your dad's so lucky to have a nutritionist for a daughter. What kind of meal plan are you making him?"

"Green juice! Trust me."

"When my dad got cancer, he went macrobiotic and how he's super-healthy."

"I saw this detox diet online . . ."

"Are you making him broth?"

"You have to get him mushrooms from this guy at the farmers market."

"He should really stop eating sugar. It feeds cancer cells."

"You should try this plant-based protein powder."

"Do you have a juicer?"

"This green tea cured my aunt's breast cancer."

"But has he tried that chemo where they turn you upside down?"

On the one hand, I was so hungry for answers to my questions about how to handle the physical and emotional logistics of helping care for my dad while still maintaining some semblance of functional human / small business owner life, but that need was quite different from the hole well-intentioned but clueless people thought they saw and tried to fill.

I was longing for someone who'd been there to tell me how they'd balanced writing deadlines and client sessions and speaking engagements with trips in and out of the city and with taking their loved one to hospitals and doctors' offices and trips to the grocery store to pick up whatever specific food that could be tolerated that week. And how did they fit in time for those simple human things like cleaning and laundry? I didn't really know who to ask, and I was worried about leaning too much on my friends, who were busy with their own responsibilities and young families.

I also just wanted someone to just ask me how I was doing. Sure, I paid my therapist to do that, but mostly I just grumbled about the subway for the first twenty minutes, then spat out whatever surface-level stuff was on my mind about my dad, peppered in an update about my attempt at a dating life or my latest work problem or success, and then spent the last ten of the forty-five minutes explaining how I just didn't have the bandwidth or income to come for more sessions each week like she kept suggesting. What could I expect to get from it, though? I was treating therapy like another item on the to-do list.

As a caregiver, chances are you'll get tons of unsolicited and terrible advice about your loved one's condition. You will probably want to smack whomever is talking to you, or you'll wish you were wearing a shirt declaring, "No Advice, Please." Totally normal.

Logically, you know that they mean well, or maybe they feel awkward and are not sure what to say. I'm sure we've all had that experience where we say something that lands as totally inane or tone-deaf about which we torture ourselves long after the moment has passed. Maybe I'm giving people too much credit (I'm told I do this a lot), but I do like to think that sometimes people just don't realize what they're saying.

Licensed Clinical Social Worker Lauren Fasanella, who spoke earlier on caregiver burnout, also has some advice for dealing with unsolicited or just bad advice. "It's always tough. I think it's one of those things where you have to separate it out. If the person is giving you advice, they are coming from a good place and mean well. You can tell them very diplomatically that what they're saying is offensive and share other ways they can be helpful, or you can ignore it and put it into the context that they're trying to be helpful. Also, remember too that you are in a very sensitive position and may be feeling a little more emotional or vulnerable and sensitive than usual."

I wish I could tell you that I kept my cool every single time someone dumped an advice bomb on me, but I also wish I could tell you that I doled out the deserved eye rolls or at least let those people know how their comments made me feel so they'd think more carefully next time they were in a situation where they felt compelled to share.

We may not be able to control what others say to us, but similarly to how we can approach stressors, we can do something about how we respond. A few of the things I personally found most helpful were:

- Take a breath before responding, verbally or nonverbally. An eye roll, sigh, or shoulder shrug can speak volumes.
- Put the "good intention" filter on and try to view their comment through that lens.
- Be mindful that when you're practicing good self-care (especially related to eating to support stable blood sugar and moving your body to keep those endorphins flowing) you'll be in a better headspace.
- It's okay to feel your feelings, but it's also okay to express them privately, such as in a journal or talking to a therapist.
- If you want to respond negatively, give yourself a moment to weigh the pros and cons of saying what's on the tip of your tongue. What do you hope will happen if you spit fire at them?
- Give yourself permission to write that person off as a jerk and avoid them (if possible) for as long as you need to cool down, be it for a few hours or forever.

CHAPTER 12

BLOOD SUGAR MANAGEMENT BASICS

Suggested Listening: "Not Fade Away"
—THE ROLLING STONES

As I introduced earlier, blood sugar management plays a huge role in our overall health and well-being. If you take away nothing else from the nutrition section of this book, let it be this: *Getting a handle on your blood sugar will make a difference in your energy, mood, and stress response.*

We tend to hear about blood sugar management in the context of diabetes risk and management, but it's vitally important to pretty much every aspect of our health and well-being. I often say that it's where everything attaches underneath. Our blood sugar balance also impacts our energy, our mood, our cognitive function, our appetite, our weight, our heart health, and our hormone function. It's also been shown to play a role in cancer risk as well as in the risk for other ailments.[4]

When you're in the role of taking care of someone (and dealing with whatever else may be going on in your life), eating to support stable blood sugar can make a huge difference in how resilient you feel. Here are some basic tips to get you started.

What to Eat to Balance Blood Sugar

It's important to have the right balance of protein, fat, and carbohydrates to support stable blood sugar. They impact blood sugar balance differently, which is why portions and proportions matter.

Short version of the story: when we eat foods that provide carbohydrates (think: grains, fruits, starchy veggies, sugar), our blood glucose rises as our body digests the starches in those foods and breaks them down into glucose, which then enters our bloodstream. Our pancreas secretes insulin to help get that glucose to the cells that need it—if this helps, think of insulin as the Amazon delivery person delivering those orders so they don't pile up in the warehouse. [vii]

When we eat carbs on an empty stomach or a disproportionately large serving when compared to fat or protein, we may get a sharp spike in blood sugar and insulin but then experience a crash, which can lead to feeling hangry and struggling with appetite control later in the day.

On a packed day when you may be taking your loved one to multiple appointments or at their bedside taking care of them, it's going to be lot harder to support stable blood sugar if you're fueling yourself primarily with vending machine snacks like candy and chips or stress-eating simple carbs like cookies. This can also happen with "healthy" carbs like fruit. Yes, an apple is a healthy food, but it may not hold you over for very long. Sure, you could have multiple pieces of fruit over the course of a day, but you'd be up and down that blood sugar roller coaster all day, which is not helpful for the mind or body.

If blood sugar remains high over time (due to diet, certain medications, stress, obesity, or a combination of factors), this can lead to insulin resistance (think of it as the cells not responding well to insulin and being, like, "Ugh, you're here *again*? Just leave that package on the porch"), which comes with its own host of health issues. [ix]

However, buffering the breakdown of those carbs by incorporating protein, fat, and fiber into your meal results in a slower digestive process, leading to a more gradual increase and then decrease in blood sugar, providing you with sustained energy and focus. At your meals and snacks, aim for a balance of protein, fat, and complex carbs spread evenly through the day. Whenever possible, I recommend being intentional about meals and snacks and having at least a loose plan if it serves you.

Here are just a few examples:

Breakfast

- whole grain toast with nut or seed butter or 1/2 an avocado with a hard-boiled egg or a tablespoon of hemp seeds on top;
- veggie omelet with fruit, whole grain toast, or roasted potatoes;
- plain Greek yogurt or cottage cheese with fruit and 1–2 tablespoons of nuts, chia seeds, or ground flax; or
- unflavored oatmeal with 1–2 tablespoons of chia seeds or ground flax topped with a tablespoon of nut or seed butter and 1 cup berries or half a banana.

Lunch and Dinner

- lentil or chicken vegetable soup and a simple side salad with oil and vinegar;

- grilled chicken breast with lettuce, tomato, and avocado on whole grain bread with sliced veggies on the side;
- a big salad with lots of veggies, protein from beans, fish, chicken, eggs, tofu, or tempeh, and some kind of healthy fat like avocado, olives, or nuts with a simple dressing of oil and vinegar or lemon juice;
- baked fish with sautéed or roasted green veggies and baked or roasted sweet potato;
- a turkey burger on a whole grain bun with a side salad. If you're craving fries, have those instead of a bun and enjoy your burger over greens;
- chili with a tablespoon of shredded cheese and / or 1/2 an avocado; or
- fajita veggies with black beans and optional chicken with guacamole and lots of salsa.

Snacks

- a piece of fruit and a piece of cheese or tablespoon of nut or seed butter;
- 3/4 cup plain Greek yogurt with 1 cup berries;
- 1/4 cup of hummus or guacamole with sliced veggies or a serving of whole grain crackers;
- 1 or 2 medjool dates stuffed with 1 tablespoon nut or seed butter;
- 3 cups popcorn with 1 tablespoon nutritional yeast;
- 1/3 cup of crispy roasted chickpeas or edamame;
- 1/4 cup of nuts or seeds;
- 1–2 hard-boiled eggs or egg white bites;
- half a PB&J sandwich on whole grain bread;
- slice of whole grain toast with half an avocado;

- 1/2 cup cooked edamame;
- 10 olives with 2 tablespoons nuts or seeds; or
- a bowl of broth-based vegetable soup with beans.

An occasional indulgence is fine and can help you avoid feeling deprived, which is helpful for staying on track with healthy eating habits for the long time. I'm a fan of an 85/15 approach to healthy eating, where the majority of what you're eating is healthful, nourishing stuff with a little room for pleasure. On an everyday basis, you want to be mindful that you're fueling your body with balanced meals and snacks. If you do want to enjoy treat foods (notice I didn't say "cheat") more often, build it into your day.

For example, if you love macaroni and cheese, rather than have a huge portion that's going to zonk you out, have a small portion along with some green veggies and consider adding extra protein like a piece of chicken. If you're making your own, play around with using legume-based pasta, which has more protein and fiber than wheat pasta. Or if mashed potatoes is your jam, have a smaller amount and load your plate with non-starchy veggies and a serving of protein. If you have a sweet tooth, experiment with pairing a little something sweet with a food that has protein and/or fat. For example, have that piece of chocolate with some nuts or cheese or alongside an unsweetened cappuccino or latte made with milk that provides protein. You could also try a few chocolate chips in yogurt or trail mix. If you love candy, have a piece at the end of a meal so it won't be a shock to your system.

How Stress Affects Blood Sugar

Stress can have a significant impact on our blood sugar, which is why nutrition can be so helpful. When we're exposed to stress, insulin levels drop as stress hormones rise, which means that insulin can't work as efficiently to lower blood sugar. When we're dealing with chronic stress, as we likely are in a caregiving role, that can lead to increases in our blood sugar for longer, setting the stage for health issues. This effect is, not surprisingly, amplified if we reach for sugary or carb-rich comfort foods that require more insulin.

There are varying opinions on this, but I tend to advise against suddenly starting a drastically different or restrictive diet when you're going through a tough time, especially if it feels really challenging or requires a ton of prep that adds to your stress level. Instead, start with one or two changes that feel doable and build on as you feel ready.

Signs of Blood Sugar Imbalance

Are you concerned that your blood sugar is imbalanced? A blood sugar test is the best way to find out for sure—a Hemoglobin A1c level, which is reflective of blood sugar control over the past three months of 5.7–6.5% is indicative of prediabetes, and above 6.5% is in the diabetes range. Even if your results are on the higher end of normal, having a conversation with your healthcare provider can be a good first step in coming up with a manageable plan get it under control and stave off future problems.[5]

Beyond labs, there are some other signs to that you may have uncontrolled blood sugar:

- feeling constantly fatigued;
- blurry vision;
- frequent headaches;
- feeling extra thirsty and having to urinate more frequently;
- skin changes like excessive dryness, blisters, sores, or skin tags; and
- frequent yeast infections.

You know yourself best, and if you notice something feels "off" please don't put off getting it checked out. You're a better caretaker to others when you take of yourself.

CHAPTER 13

STRESS, INFLAMMATION, AND DIET

Suggested Listening: "Burned"
—BUFFALO SPRINGFIELD

E arlier I touched on the inflammatory effect stress can have on the body and the role of nutrition, so wanted to loop in a functional medicine doctor on the topic. I really like Dr. Will Cole's description of inflammation in the body (especially chronic inflammation) as a "check engine" light. Dr. Cole, who is a leading functional medicine expert and author of *Ketotarian*, *The Inflammation Spectrum*, and *Intuitive Fasting*, describes it as a sign to figure out what is going on in the body that's causing those inflammatory symptoms.

Some early signs of inflammation (including stress-related) he most commonly sees in patients in his practice often include:

- brain fog;
- fatigue;
- digestive problems;
- skin issues like rashes and breakouts;
- musculoskeletal tightness;
- poor immune system function; and
- background anxiousness.

"With anxiety, if someone is a caregiver, often it's situational," but especially when they are in that role for a prolonged period of time, that rise in inflammation can become chronic, and if they aren't aware of what lifestyle approaches can help or aren't prioritizing their eating, sleep, and other supportive practices, "it's a perfect storm" for a larger health problem.

Reframe Your Relationship with Stress
"Lumping all stress together and making them all bad is not fair—some stress is okay, and there *is* good stress." However, the effect on the body can be very different. "Sometimes there will be times in our life when stress is higher," said Dr. Cole, "but that's when you need to focus on those little self-care practices."

When you're not in control of the stress, Dr. Cole recommends shifting your relationship with it. "You're almost making friends with it. If you can't change it or leave it, you have to accept it and move through it with as much grace as possible." Focus on doing what you can to be more resilient in the face of stress. Making mindful (and sustainable) choices with your food and lifestyle habits, even if it's just a few small things, can make a difference.

Foods That Contribute to Inflammation
It's been well established that certain foods can contribute to inflammation, while others counteract it. When it comes to the foods that trigger inflammation, looking at it through the lens of bio-individuality (the concept that there is no "one size fits all" approach to health and wellness), know that this effect can vary from person to person. You may even find that you're affected more at some times (like during times of stress) than at others because of how factors like stress impact the body's functioning, including metabolism of nutrients.

For example, you may find that you crash more quickly if you have carbs without enough fat or protein, or you may feel like you don't digest certain foods as well—it's not your imagination. As I shared earlier, I went through that myself after my adventures in sleep deprivation and antibiotics, feeling more sensitive to grains (to the point where I needed to take a break), and I even found that my nut allergy extended to new sensitivities to peanuts and coconut. That is not necessarily a normal response, but if you've been through something similar and think you're crazy or that it's in your head, honor what you're feeling and check in with your healthcare provider.

When we got on the topic of foods to avoid, Dr. Cole explained, "I don't mean to oversimplify and say everyone has to avoid these all of the time." What is important to keep in mind, though, is that "If your cup's already overflowing as a caregiver because you're going through a stressful time, these foods may play a bigger role in that overflow because your resilience threshold is already low."

A big part of the mechanism through which those foods spark inflammation often has to do with disruption of the gut microbiome (which, as we'll talk more about in another chapter, is where most of our immune system function happens) and that food's impact on blood sugar and insulin levels (a major factor in inflammation).

Here are a few of the most common culprits. It's possible for someone to react to a food not on this list, so in general, just pay attention to how you feel:

Added Sugars. Sugar can wreak havoc on our blood sugar, setting us up for a roller coaster-like experience when it comes to blood sugar balance. Not helpful for dealing with stress. "Even the insidious and wholesome sounding ones," explained Dr. Cole, can be problematic. "Marketing campaigns can make it sound more natural, but it will still impact blood sugar and insulin and disrupt the microbiome. With the data we have, natural sugar alternatives and sugar alcohols are a better alternative, but some may still be irritating to the gut. Used sparingly as a treat, it can be okay, just as long as it's not all day every day. Quality matters, but generally speaking, I do like them better. The one caveat to that would be honey and maple syrup, which do impact blood sugar, but used sparingly, I would put them on the same playing field." Like Dr. Cole, I tell my patients to treat sugar alternatives as they would regular sugar. Choose the sweetener that actually satisfies you and be mindful about the amount.

Refined Grains. Because the body breaks down refined flours so quickly (think white bread, white pasta, and the like), they can contribute to unstable blood sugar levels. When possible, choose higher-fiber options to slow the digestive process.

Certain Grains. "We have to be nuanced and specific. I don't mean to demonize all grains, but how you prepare them and the quality of the grain matters," said Dr. Cole. He noted that gluten-containing grains (such as wheat, barley, and rye or oats that are contaminated with wheat, a common issue in United States agriculture) tend to be the most common ones people have difficulty with. Some people may also find that, if they are more sensitive to carbohydrates as a result of the body's response to stress and its impact on blood sugar, they find that it doesn't really matter whether that grain contains gluten or not.

Red and Processed Meat. Many studies have linked red and processed meat to inflammation as well as cancer and heart disease. Part of this has to do with their high saturated fat content and prolonged digestion time, and, in the case of processed meat, it is also related to compounds created during salting, curing, and smoking processes.[6]

Industrial Seed Oils. Certain industrial seed oils such as canola, vegetable oil, and soybean oil, have been linked to inflammation due to their high levels of omega-6 fatty acids. While we do need some omega-6, having too much (something which is very easy to do on a standard American diet) compared to omega-3 fatty acid, has been associated with inflammation as well. If you're reading this and freaking out because your favorite hummus has canola oil listed as an ingredient, don't panic. "Some people are okay with small amounts, but some react to small amounts," said Dr. Cole. What I usually tell my patients is that, if that oil is an ingredient in something you eat occasionally and it's just a little, you are most likely fine, but for things that are a staple in your diet, I do recommend swapping in an oil noted to have anti-inflammatory benefits, such as olive oil or avocado oil.

Trans Fats. The one fat I tell my patients to flat-out avoid whenever possible is trans fat, which is created via hydrogenation, usually to change the texture of a fat to make it more solid at room temperature. Hydrogenated oils in products like shortening and margarine are examples, and foods made with these hydrogenated fats. Trans fats contribute to inflammation by lowering HDL ("good") cholesterol and raising the LDL ("bad") cholesterol, both of which are independently linked to increased risk of heart disease, stroke, and diabetes. Checking an ingredient label is a good way to tell if that food has trans fat: look for hydrogenated or partially hydrogenated oils. There is a one-gram limit that manufacturers have to stay under, so if you do choose to consume a food that has some trans fat, stick to a small portion.

Certain Dairy Products. Though Dr. Cole pointed out that not everyone needs to avoid all dairy products forever, quality does matter. "You can get better versions that are more tolerable than conventional dairy, such as A2 milk, organic, grass-fed, and fermented dairy products." You are the expert on you, so pay attention to how your body responds to different types and amounts of dairy. For example, you may find that you feel better using a plant-based milk in recipes and foods like smoothies but tolerate fermented dairy like yogurt and kefir or small amounts of low-lactose cheese.

Eating to Fight Inflammation

When it comes to fighting inflammation with food, what you do eat matters just as much as what you don't. Marketing campaigns have a way of making us think we need to be dropping serious cash on supplements and superfood-fortified snack foods, but you can find lots of what you need at your local grocery store. Fill up on nutrient-rich fruits and veggies (frozen is completely okay, by the way—the freezing process locks in a lot of the nutritional value), healthy fats like olive oil, nuts and seeds, and avocado, and minimally processed proteins like wild fish and organic poultry. Consuming adequate fiber can help keep digestion regular and support overall wellness (more on that in another chapter).

If you're strapped for time to cook and want to stick to a budget, meal prepping can come in handy. "If you are spending money on snacks through the week in a reactionary way or going out to eat a lot," it can add up in terms of how it impacts your body and your bank account, "but if you plan ahead, you can make the most out of your grocery haul."

It doesn't have to be anything fancy, either. Dr. Cole frequently recommends simple soups and stews to his patients. "Even just batch-cooking can go a long way too and can help with your gut health."

Lifestyle Factors That Matter

While important, food is not the only factor. As we've talked about, stress is one of the more obvious contributors. That said, Dr. Cole cautions against stressing about your stress and what it may be doing to your well-being—that's just piling on additional stress. "The body is incredibly resilient," said Dr. Cole. "You can be pragmatic and practical in this season of life, but don't stress about not stressing or stress too much about eating healthy, even. Go easy on yourself and do the best you can. There's a certain level of grit humans can take. Some things you can change, some things you can't, so approach it like, 'I'm going through a stressful time and I want to manage what I *can* manage.'" While stress can worsen chronic inflammation, being a perfectionist about your stress management and beating yourself up about what you're not doing or still struggling with can be just as detrimental.

Focus on what you can do. It may be hard to be okay with being where you are, but when you feel overwhelmed, says Dr. Cole, "I think we need to look at what we *do* have agency over in this season of life. We need to look at even the small margins of our life and see, what are the small things we can bring into our life? Can you get out in nature? Can you optimize sleep because it is powerfully restorative? Maybe it's downloading a mindfulness app and doing it for five or ten minutes a day."

Use technology mindfully. This would be a good time to cultivate a more balanced relationship with your electronics and re-assess your news and social media habits. "Another thing most people can do is to decrease the amount of technology they bring in and set healthy boundaries with their phone. If you're looking at your phone scrolling and taking in that blue light, it can disrupt melatonin and sleep quality."

Seek Social Support. That saying, "You can't pour from an empty cup" is a cliché for a reason. Additionally, loneliness and isolation have also been associated with increased disease risk. "You can only give what you have, and if your health is depleting, you can only give so much." Having a support system is key to helping you avoid getting to that totally burnt-out point. "I see a lot of people declining when they are serving as caretakers. You need to have a healthy support system."

Part of that process of assembling your support team, explains Dr. Cole, is telling people what you need. "What I hear from patients is, 'My friends have things going on. I don't want to worry them.' They don't know what you need until you speak up." An area where technology can be helpful, though? Scheduling a virtual catch-up with friends or joining an online support group.

This support team can include licensed professionals too. Sometimes seeking professional help, like that of a mental healthcare practitioner, can be incredibly helpful, especially if you're dealing with any past traumas that get activated by the stress you're currently under.

Optimize Your Sleep. You've heard it before and will hear it again: sleep is an incredibly important piece of the picture when you're trying to get or keep the mind and body in balance during times of stress. We'll talk about this in more detail in later chapters, but a few basic (and inexpensive) practices that can help are to stop using technology before bed or wear blue light blocking glasses. You can also check out free sleep content online or on an app (yes, more technology, but you don't have to look at the screen for things like meditation and ambient sound.) Essential oil diffusers can also be found inexpensively if you want to incorporate relaxing aromatherapy into your sleep routine.

Spend time in nature. "Getting out in nature is completely free," says Dr. Cole. We have lots of research on the many benefits of getting healthy amounts of exposure to sunlight and greenery: "Just getting some fresh sunlight and fresh air can be therapeutic." Nature can also be a part of a grounding (pun intended) spiritual or mindfulness practice to help heal the parasympathetic nervous system to get back into a "rest and digest" place.

CHAPTER 14

THE FOOD-MOOD CONNECTION

Suggested Listening: "Where Is My Mind?"
—PIXIES

"Stress eating" and "emotional eating" are terms used to describe eating in response to stress or unpleasant emotions—they usually have a negative connotation and refer to eating unhealthy food or eating compulsively when stressed or emotional. However, we can reframe that and examine how what we eat can have a meaningful impact on our mood and our stress response. Something I counsel my patients on—and have found tremendously helpful in my own life—is incorporating foods that have been noted to help promote a more stable mood and keeping an eye toward fueling the body and mind to be resilient.

When you're dealing with a lot of responsibilities and difficult emotions on a day-to-day basis, it can be hard to feel motivated to eat healthier if you're used to food choices being about weight management or appearance or because you read somewhere that it's what you "should" be doing. When you shift your mindset to making it about how what you eat can improve how you feel, that adds a lot of value and may help you tap more easily into your "why" at mealtimes.

The Gut-Brain Connection

The gastrointestinal system (aka, "the gut") and our brain are connected. We have a second brain in our gut, so to speak, called the enteric nervous system (ENS), which is made up of[7] millions of sensory neurons, motor neurons, interneurons, and enteric glia (cells that regulate homeostasis in the GI tract) embedded in the gastrointestinal wall, starting in the lower third of the esophagus and going all the way down through the rectum. There are two layers of the ENS: the submucosal (which is primarily involved with water regulation, electrolyte secretion, and blood flow), and the myenteric plexus (responsible for helping coordinate movements throughout the gut).[8]

The ENS and the Central Nervous System (CNS) continuously "talk" to each other via cell signaling. The vagus nerve is a major player in this process. One of twelve cranial nerves (nerve X, if you're curious) that help link the brain to other parts of the body, it runs all the way from the brain stem to the colon. Its digestive functions involve playing a role in stimulating movement the esophagus, stomach, and intestines. It also is involved with taste sensation near the root of the tongue, and with stimulating muscles in the larynx, pharynx, and soft palate. It also is involved in stimulating muscles in the heart to help lower heart rate.

When the vagus nerve is damaged, some of the digestive issues someone may experience include nausea, vomiting, bloating, abdominal pain, gastroparesis, or difficulty swallowing. Changes in blood pressure or heart rate may also occur. When the vagus nerve overreacts to a stress trigger, it can cause a sudden drop in blood pressure and heart rate, causing you to pass out—this is called vasovagal syncope.

Vagus nerve stimulation, on the flip side, is sometimes used as a treatment for cases of epilepsy or depression in which other treatments have not been successful.

The term "nervous stomach" relates to the fact that the autonomic nervous system (in particular, the parasympathetic nervous system) regulates digestion. A troubled mind can trouble the stomach, and gastrointestinal issues have also been associated with mental stress and mood changes. If you've ever noticed that you get diarrhea or constipation when you're upset or stressed—or if you've noticed you just don't feel yourself when your digestion is off—that's the gut-brain connection at work.

Food and Mood

One of my absolute favorite topics (besides music) to nerd out on is the food-mood connection. Dr. Uma Naidoo is the Harvard-trained nutritional psychiatrist, professional chef, nutrition specialist, and author of the national best seller: *This Is Your Brain on Food: An Indispensable Guide to the Surprising Foods that Fight Depression, Anxiety, PTSD, OCD, ADHD, and More.*

She describes nutritional psychiatry as the use of healthy whole foods with nutrients to improve how you're feeling emotionally, your mental fitness, and your overall well-being. "Our body intelligence is one of the key indicators that empowers us because it involves us listening to our body and using that information to our health advantage." There are also foods that can have a negative impact on our mental and emotional well-being. "When our brain is in that stress mode and we reach for comfort foods, those comfort foods are actually discomfort foods for the brain." On the other end of the spectrum, certain foods can improve our mental state.

You can get much more information in her book, but here are some of the highlights we spoke about.

What Not to Eat

Dr. Naidoo recommends limiting foods that have been shown to contribute to inflammation and/or mess with our blood sugar levels, as these are known factors that may worsen your emotional state. You will find more on foods to avoid for each mental health condition in her book, but here are a few major ones:

- refined sugars;
- most artificial sweeteners;
- processed and ultra-processed foods; and
- processed / refined vegetable / seed oils.

Check nutrition labels and remember that refined sugar has many, many names. And go slow with even more wholesome-sounding sweeteners, as many can still spike your blood sugar and insulin and negatively impact your mood. Many artificial sweeteners aren't helping much either. One of the reasons to limit them is that they can train our taste buds to expect high levels of sweetness and may increase sugar cravings.

While there are many reasons to limit processed foods, from a brain health standpoint, explains Dr. Naidoo, "We also know that processed foods cause problems," thanks to ingredients like unhealthy trans fats, sugar, and refined vegetable oils, preservatives, colorants, stabilizers, and dyes which have been associated with inflammation, now a major factor underlying mental health conditions.[9]

Fill Up on These

Certain foods are your allies in mood management and stress response. Here are a few of the few that Dr. Naidoo highlights as a starting place:

High-Fiber Foods. "Fiber-filled foods are your friends when you're anxious because they break down more slowly and don't cause an insulin spike. You feel satiated for longer and don't get those jittery feelings." Sure, a sugary treat may be tempting, she says, but "when someone eats a sugary donut, they don't realize it's also spiking their insulin," which can then spike anxiety. Just be mindful to reach for foods that are naturally high in fiber and not processed foods with fiber added to make them seem healthier. A few nourishing examples are vegetables, high-fiber fruits like berries and apples, legumes, nuts, seeds, and whole grains.

Vitamin D–rich foods. Vitamin D status plays a role in depression, as it is involved in various brain processes. Research has found an association between low vitamin D levels and depression. Vitamin D receptors have been found on glias and neurons in areas of the brain that are thought to be part of the pathophysiology of depression.[10] To get the recommended 600–800 IU/day, Dr. Naidoo recommends eating foods like oily fish, pastured eggs, fortified grass-fed dairy products, and mushrooms or to consider a supplement to help you cover your bases.

Spices. "Cooking with spices is more than just delicious, it's a way to help support a better mood," says Dr. Naidoo. Her go-to? Turmeric with a pinch of black pepper to enhance absorption. "I ask people to incorporate 1/4 teaspoon of turmeric into their day. Try it in a tea or a smoothie to start if you're not cooking." Dried is fine. If you're cooking with it, she recommends adding it to a stir-fry or other mixed dish.[11]

Omega-3s. These polyunsaturated fatty acids have been shown in numerous studies to help with anxiety. EPA and DHA are the two omega-3s found in animal sources (primarily oily fish like salmon, tuna, mackerel, and sardines), while the plant-based ALA can be found in certain foods, such as flax seeds, chia seeds, and walnuts. Just note that you would need to eat more of these, as the ALA undergoes an additional process in the body to become DHA. There is currently no standardized requirement of omega-3s, but the recommended adequate intake (AI) of ALA is 1.1–1.6 grams per day.[12]

Magnesium-Rich Foods. Magnesium is a mineral that plays an important role in a wide variety of body processes, including muscle and nerve function and which has also been linked in studies to reduced anxiety. One of the reasons it may help with anxiety, researchers believe, is that it may improve brain function by helping regulate neurotransmitters and cell signaling and assist with brain functions that reduce stress and anxiety.[13] A few of Dr. Naidoo's favorite sources are chickpeas and pumpkin seeds "because they are easy to add" to dishes. She also recommends avocados—in addition to providing magnesium, they're also a good source of healthy fat and fiber.

What to Eat When You're Totally Burnt Out

When you're feeling burnt out, getting back to basics and being reminded of the helpful habits that can make a difference is important. Dr. Naidoo explains, "When someone is feeling down-trodden and has reached that point, you need to foster awareness. Things I like to remind them of are hydration, anti-inflammatory foods, and antioxidant rich-foods and how to include those in their diet. For example, when you're eating a colorful salad with a rainbow of vegetables, it's rich in fiber, rich in antioxidants, and will help you reset and help your body repair itself."

She states that many people don't realize they're stressed and that caregivers are especially susceptible to burnout—they're focused on being a caregiver who is on demand all the time. Functioning at that level, she explains, spikes their stress level, which spikes their cortisol. "We want to help them reset and to pay attention to self-care." She recommends starting simple. "Make sure you start with a healthy breakfast and that you're well hydrated." If you're on the go a lot, for example, driving the person you're caring for to appointments or have a lot of demands placed on you, reminding yourself that incorporating healthy eating habits into your day can sustain you and help you be a better caregiver.

"Think of this as helping yourself to take care of them," she says. "In a caregiver role, it's easy to think, 'I need to take care of my loved one' but not yourself." Remind yourself that nurturing yourself is important for understanding the role you're in and for reframing your thoughts to be more self-compassionate. If you're motivated by being reminded of what will happen if you *don't* care for yourself, Dr. Naidoo adds that "stress can impact your gut and set you up for inflammation" and the health issues that can come with that, including worsening of mental health symptoms.

What to Eat for Better Sleep

With sleep, admits Dr. Naidoo, "it's not just one thing. It's many of the things that are going on during your day. There's the obvious, like coffee, and another is not relying on wine to get to sleep." If you're doing to drink, she says, "have it earlier in the day if you are struggling with insomnia."

What you have for dinner can make a difference too. Have breakfast for dinner! "Eggs have melatonin," Dr. Naidoo explains. She's a big fan of a vegetable omelet for dinner, for those that eat eggs. Plant-based sources include barley, rolled oats, grapes, pomegranates, walnuts, sunflower seeds, and flaxseeds to help get your body ready for sleep.

Another of her favorite melatonin-containing foods is tart cherries, which are available in fresh, frozen, or juice form. Just be mindful that if you're using the juice form, watch out for added sugar and keep an eye on portion size. "If they get the juice, I will have them have ¼ cup or so about a half hour before they go to sleep. If they haven't had it before, I want them to start with a little bit. Most people don't need much and do feel sleepy. Eating the actual cherries, I always go with a ¼ cup. Many people struggle with weight as a result of psychiatric medication so we start with low glycemic foods." She recommends enjoying them as a small snack to ease into bed about thirty to sixty minutes before turning in for the night.

Find Ways to Make Mood-Boosting Eating Convenient

Eating to support a better mood doesn't have to be complicated. Dr. Naidoo says, "I always tell my patients about things they may not realize are healthy options, like frozen products. I usually say to them avoid extra sodium, syrups, or added sugar, and to look at the label." Cooking can be simple too. "Steaming vegetables and adding a squeeze of lemon to add a couple side dishes to your main is nice. You can also roast them."

She also recommends doing a little meal prep on a day where you have an hour or two free. It will help simplify the week ahead and can be helpful whether you have a family or are single. "Or some people prefer to use a crock pot or slow cooker they don't have to manage," she adds. For easy breakfast options, she encourages exploring make-ahead breakfasts like overnight oats that you don't really have to do much with. "There are also things like chia pudding they can make ahead to use as a snack or breakfast."

There are a lot of healthy and convenient options to be found on supermarket shelves as well. "Things I recommend from the supermarket are frozen fruits and vegetables, canned organic beans (just drain the liquid and rinse them before use). For omega-3s, wild sockeye salmon is something you can easily add to a salad or have with roasted vegetables." While you may have been told in the past to only "shop the perimeter" of the store and avoid the aisles, there actually are nutritious items to be found there. "There are things in the aisles that are good brain foods," says Dr. Naidoo, "like lentils (high fiber), canned mussels and clams are high in zinc, canned mackerel and sardines are high in omega-3s."

Look at the Habits You "Feed" Yourself With

Food is an important piece of the picture, but it's not the whole picture.

"I like people to understand," says Dr. Naidoo, "that there is more than one way to work on stress. Food is one, but there are more." She also counsels her patients on incorporating lifestyle habits "like meditation or mindfulness or listening to music or sounds." She also supports the use of apps such as breathing apps and relaxation apps. "I lead with food," she says, "but I also like people to think about other integrative and functional ways of managing stress. When someone needs to work on their stress, we need to use several modalities. One may be able to do tai chi, another may do yoga, another may do meditation" in addition to working on their diet.

"I feel that caregivers need to understand that it's not selfish to take care of themselves. They should have some kind of practice that grounds them in their role and prepares them for what they have to face in a day. Whether that is how they wake up, recite a prayer, or write in a gratitude journal or meditate—they should make sure they have a good self-care plan."

In *This Is Your Brain on Food*, Dr. Naidoo touches on her own experience as a cancer survivor and shares how supporting herself with dietary approaches to managing her anxiety helped her through chemotherapy treatment.

"When you are a patient," she said to me, "you have a lot of worries." When asked how caregivers can be helpful to someone who is going through treatment or living with a medical issue, she replied, "To be openly supportive. What I can say is that my friends and family around me, when they were scared about what I was going through, they didn't reflect that back to me. It helped to strengthen my resolve and to know that I could lean on them emotionally. They had a lot of emotions, but they managed them through their own supports and were very supportive of me, which gave me a lot of strength."

The second thing that made a difference, she said, was that they helped her feel that life was normal. "Even though they might be driving me to chemotherapy or taking me out to eat when I was able to do that, they would act like it was normal. They tried to make it as normal as possible for me, and I really appreciated that. The last thing I wanted to feel was that I was in that patient role. It helped me feel empowered to go out with a friend for dinner and do what we would normally do. Because of fatigue, it was usually shorter and earlier in the day but it still really helped."

The spirituality of the people in her life also played a role. "Whether they were Buddhist, Jewish—my family is Hindu—whatever their spiritual center. Everyone brought in their prayers and sense of spirituality which was a very big support for me."

CHAPTER 15

NURTURE YOUR GUT HEALTH

Suggested Listening: "I Ain't the Same"
—ALABAMA SHAKES

I couldn't include a nutrition section in this book and not talk about nurturing gut health. As discussed earlier in the book, the connection between our gastrointestinal system and mental and emotional health is an important one. The state of our gut health also impacts our immune system function, our energy, and numerous other aspects of our well-being.

I spoke with Dr. Vincent Pedre, MD, internist, functional medicine certified practitioner, and author of the best-selling book *Happy Gut*. When asked how he would describe a healthy gut, he said, "A healthy gut is a gut that basically does its work in the background without talking back to you. You're not getting rumbling, bloating, or abdominal pain. You eat your food, you feel full for about twenty minutes and it passes and feels like everything is digesting properly. You don't get that bloated feeling, you go to the bathroom regularly (once or twice a day), and those bowel movements are somewhere between firm and soft (but not diarrhea)."

One caveat, he added, "is that if you have good digestion but have a lot of what I call 'gut related health issues' such as hives, eczema, joint aches, fatigue, and mental fog, you may still have an unhealthy gut. You don't have to have gut symptoms to have gut problems. Unlike Las Vegas, he added, what happens in the gut doesn't just stay in the gut.

To help illustrate how important the health of our gut is to our overall well-being, he said, "The gut is the cornerstone of your health; the cornerstone is the stone that was laid first to determine the orientation of a building. The gut is the foundation of your health. You wouldn't build a house without a foundation, and you can't build your health without a healthy gut foundation."

Signs of an unhealthy gut may include but are not limited to:

- digestive discomfort (ex: gas, bloating, constipation, diarrhea, abdominal pain, etc.);
- acne;
- allergies;
- anxiety;
- autoimmune issues;
- brain fog;
- depression;
- fatigue;
- nutrient deficiencies;
- rashes (eczema, psoriasis, etc.); and
- unexpected weight changes.

These symptoms may range from mildly annoying to incredibly disruptive. A lot of them can also be reflective of other health conditions and therefore easy to dismiss as symptoms of issues with the gastrointestinal system. You know yourself best, and if something just doesn't feel right, Dr. Pedre explains, "You ask yourself 'what else'— what else is going on, what else can I do?" That first step can be reaching out to your healthcare provider to talk about what you're experiencing.

Healing Gut Issues

In an unhealthy gut, the equilibrium of that gut microbiome is disturbed, causing a variety of issues. I know it's easy to quickly start trying to think of all the things you're "doing wrong," but there are lots of reasons gut health may become compromised. Yes, sometimes a poor-quality diet, high alcohol intake, or unhealthy habits that trigger inflammation may be the cause, but it can be other stuff that is way beyond our control. For example, certain medications (especially antibiotics); stress; an underlying health issue like a virus, a parasite, or worm; an undiagnosed food sensitivity; or environmental toxins or irritants may be the root cause.

While the exact path to healing will look different from one person to the next, one of the primary goals of that healing process is to bring the gut back into balance, often through dietary changes as a key part of that process. A damaged gut may have a hard time digesting anything properly, Dr. Pedre explains, so while their initial regimen may be more restricted, they likely will be able to reintroduce some things over time.

Some foods that are often limited on a gut-healing plan include:

- wheat (especially in people who are sensitive);
- dairy (in people who are sensitive);
- sugar;
- artificial sweeteners and other sugar substitutes like monk fruit and stevia;
- sugar alcohols (xylitol, erythritol);
- fried foods;

- red meat; and
- legumes, corn, and soy, for people who are sensitive
  to lectins.

All that said, triggers can vary from one person to the next, so other foods may be limited if it is believed that they are causing digestive problems. Sometimes after a period of elimination, small amounts will be gradually reintroduced to see if that person can tolerate them once their gut has healed.

I strongly recommend working with a licensed healthcare practitioner who specializes in gut health for guidance. This work can be very specific and nuanced, and you really can't get that level of individualized care from a website or social media influencer. I can't tell you how many times I've seen someone cutting out tons of things from their diet and still feel miserable, only to later find out that the root cause was something else entirely. I understand that when you are in a caregiver role, it can feel like, "When the hell am I going to have time to focus on gut health?" Start by having a conversation with your doctor to help determine what an approachable way to start addressing your issues would be.

What to eat when healing your gut will vary from one individual to the next, but some common foods you'll see included as part of a gut-healing diet are:

- Polyphenol-rich foods and beverages like fruit, vegetables, cacao, and unsweetened tea.
- Bone broth (Dr. Pedre favors the really thick, gelatinous varieties for helping to heal the gut lining) or mushroom-based broths. Broths have been used medicinally for thousands of years for a variety of conditions. While some question their role in restoring gut lining, if nothing else, they can be a

gentle way to incorporate protein, vitamins, and minerals while hydrating.

- Nut, oat, or legume-based milks used in place of dairy.
- Healthy fats like olive oil, avocado oil, and fresh avocado (if someone can tolerate its fiber content).
- Wild salmon and other wild-caught fish high in omega-3 fatty acids.
- Healing spices like turmeric and ginger incorporated into cooking (if tolerated—these sometimes need to be introduced later in the healing process).
- Fermented foods to provide beneficial probiotic bacteria, unless contraindicated as in the case of very strong gut dysbiosis or yeast overgrowth. Some good food sources that are readily available include sauerkraut, kimchi, yogurt, kefir, and kombucha tea. For someone who needs to go slow with adding fermented foods, Dr. Pedre will often have them start with just a teaspoon of sauerkraut juice or kefir, either plant-based or organic dairy-based, increasing slowly over time. Because the bacteria in the kefir consume most of the lactose in kefir, he explains, it may still be well tolerated by people who generally are lactose intolerant. While kombucha does provide probiotics, you need to be mindful of the sugar content when buying a commercial brand. Stick with just a small amount at a time.

A Little More on Probiotics

Probiotic bacteria are beneficial gut bacteria that help promote gut health by fighting off invading pathogens and promoting regular digestion. Probiotics are found in fermented foods such as yogurt, kefir, sauerkraut, kimchi, kombucha (a fermented tea drink), pickled vegetables, miso, and tempeh. Different foods provide different types of probiotic bacteria, and these different bacteria have different effects on the body. For example, certain strains have been noted to have impacts on bloating, or easing diarrhea, whereas others have been noted for benefits to immune system function or brain health.[14] Because these bacteria have a pretty short lifespan, it's important to regularly repopulate through food or supplements. That said, many healthcare professionals point out that it is very hard to get what you need from food and recommend supplementing to ensure you're covering your bases, and to choose a product with a variety of strains. Touch base with your doctor to see if a probiotic is right for you and which product to choose.

What About Prebiotics?

Prebiotics are a very importance piece of the gut health picture because they provide fuel for those probiotics. Prebiotics are essentially indigestible fibers found in foods such as apples, asparagus, bananas, garlic, flax, leeks, onions, oats, Jerusalem artichoke, chicory root, and wheat bran. Because cooking can alter these fibers, it's recommended that you enjoy them raw (when it makes sense) or use a very light cooking method like steaming. To get the most bang for your buck, consume probiotics and prebiotics at the same time. A few real-life examples of this may include:

- plain yogurt with ground flax mixed in;
- a kefir smoothie made with banana;
- overnight oats made with kefir; and
- a grain bowl with lightly cooked asparagus, sautéed onions, and garlic topped with sauerkraut.

Just as a heads-up, some people may find that certain prebiotic-rich foods may cause gas or abdominal discomfort. Pay attention to how various foods and combinations of foods affect you. If you're new to having more fiber in your day, stepping it up gradually and drinking a little extra water can help alleviate digestive issues.

Symbiotics

A symbiotic product is one that provides both probiotics and prebiotics to make it easier to get the benefit of combining the two. Look for a product with a variety of probiotic bacteria strains and avoid lots of additives.

Postbiotics

At the time of the writing of this book, there is no official definition for postbiotics, but they have been described as bioactive compounds produced during the fermentation process of a food or beverage that provide a benefit to the host's gastrointestinal system.[15] During the fermentation that results during digestion, certain metabolites are formed, and some of these—the postbiotics—have been shown to have potential benefits antioxidant, anti-inflammatory, and antimicrobial effects, to name a few.[16] What's especially appealing about these compounds (besides their potential benefits) is that they don't have to be kept alive the way probiotic bacteria do. For example, while cooking may deactivate probiotic bacteria, the metabolites still present in that food after cooking may still be beneficial to the gut.

Lifestyle Factors in Gut Health

Because the gut and the brain are so connected, certain lifestyle practices can also help support gut health. I've seen (and honestly, experienced myself) times where someone is checking all the boxes in regard to food and exercise but is still struggling.

"I call stress the elephant in the room, especially when it comes to gut health," says Dr. Pedre. "Stress is like an attack on your gut. When you think you're checking all the boxes but are still stressed and stuck in your Type A lifestyle with no room for rest and recovery, you're not going to heal your gut."

Some great ways he recommends to de-stress and to help you get into the flow and parasympathetic state of rest and digestion may include:

- meditation;
- yoga;
- tai chi;
- qigong;
- walking in nature;
- going to the beach;
- doing a hobby you enjoy;
- playing music;
- painting; or
- spending time on other creative pursuits just for the joy of it.

CHAPTER 16

MAKE IT CONVENIENT
TO EAT WELL

Suggested Listening: "Watching the Wheels (acoustic)"
—JOHN LENNON

You can have the best meal plan in the world, but if you can't stick to it, it's not going to work for you. So often, I see people make it a story about willpower when they fail to stay on track with a healthy eating routine, but 99.9% of the time, it's not about willpower at all. In most cases, that pattern they were trying to follow just wasn't a good fit.

When it comes to diet (especially if there is a goal like weight loss involved) we're conditioned to think that extreme changes are the only way to see progress. In reality, it tends to be the tiny tweaks and subtle shifts that lead to lasting change. Something that's also easy to lose sight of is that maintenance totally counts as success, especially when you're juggling a lot more than usual or going through a stressful time. No matter your specific goal (even if that goal is maintenance), the best way to be consistent with healthy eating is to make it convenient as possible for yourself. Here are some of my favorite ways to do so:

Focus on just a few things at a time. Sure, maybe there are a few changes you'd like to make, but it really is okay to start with a tiny thing that will make a meaningful difference to you or that will just be doable. For example, maybe you know you want to work on eating more vegetables, cutting back on red meat, and drinking more water, but the only one that seems feasible is to drink water—start there. Giving yourself the chance to master something will build your confidence.

Get specific. To stick with the water example, get clear first on why you struggle. Is it forgetting to drink? Is it not liking the taste of water? Is it being worried about having to use the restroom when you have to be in the car a long time or taking your loved one to a lot of appointments and not wanting to leave them alone? Something else? From there, start brainstorming solutions for those specifics and pick one approach to try first.

Embrace shortcuts. A lack of time and energy to shop for and prepare meals prevents many caregivers from eating well. If the idea of cooking from scratch at the end of a long day or early in the morning can feel overwhelming, utilize shortcuts like frozen produce, prepared proteins (canned beans, hard boiled eggs, precooked fish, chicken, and tofu), and vegetable sides. Healthier frozen entrees and canned soup can be helpful too.

There are also lots of meal kit and meal delivery services available to suit a wide variety of needs and preferences. While some can be costly, if it's going to make a meaningful difference in your physical and mental well-being (and save you from leaning on unhealthy coping mechanisms) the time savings and benefit to your well-being can be valuable. If committing to a service on the regular isn't financially feasible, one option is to treat yourself to a shipment as an occasional treat or if you have a week coming up you know is going to be hell on wheels.

Pack what you need. If you know you've got a busy day ahead, the night before or early that morning set aside some snacks and pack a few easy items like sandwiches and bottled water. One thing we found really useful when first getting used to what was available at and around the hospital where my dad got most of his care was packing a cooler. It saved a ton of time and stress.

The goal is to keep your energy up and your mood as stable as possible via blood sugar control, so aim for a balance of protein, fat, and complex carbs. For example, some good transportable protein options are hard boiled eggs, nuts and seeds, plain Greek yogurt, cooked chicken, meat, or tofu. Sandwiches made on whole grain bread are convenient and affordable. Try nut butter and fruit or hummus and veggies. Speaking of veggies, sliced vegetables and cherry tomatoes make a great vehicle for hummus or guacamole. You can also snack on dried vegetable chips to help boost your intake when there aren't a lot of convenient or appealing options nearby. For sweet snacks that will give you energy, pack fruit or stash some minimally processed protein bars made from nuts and dried fruit. While they sound more like breakfast, overnight oats, chia pudding, and baked oatmeal are all very convenient options. Don't forget to pack napkins, utensils, and water!

And if you're, like, "Okay, I am *not* packing a cooler," maybe you'll like the next tip a little better.

Keep a list of healthy takeout options. Takeout doesn't have to automatically equal "unhealthy." A mindset shift that's been helpful for my clients and patients over the years is to remember that, with the same five minutes they spend ordering a meal they'll feel crummy after, they can order something that will be nourishing and energizing. If you feel too overwhelmed by the idea of trying a new place (been there), start with places you already tend to order from.

For one example, if you're getting Italian, look beyond the pasta and see if there's a grilled or baked fish or chicken dish that sounds good. Or try bean soup and a green salad. If you're having sushi, consider sashimi and a salad, or try swapping brown rice for white to at least get some more fiber. When having Chinese, opt for a steamed or stir-fried option that's not breaded and go heavy on the veggies, not on the rice and noodles. One of my family's go-to options for a quick meal was diners, which can be great because their menus are huge. It's just as easy to order grilled chicken with a side of veggies or an omelet or a bowl of soup as it is to order a bacon cheeseburger deluxe. If having a physical list (electronic or paper) will help you remember what your favorite healthy options are so you're less likely to make a knee-jerk choice when exhausted or stressed, jot them down somewhere you'll see them. The Notes application on your phone is especially great for this.

Outsource what you can. I understand that this one can sometimes feel especially challenging because it involves asking for help and / or spending money. Start by thinking of what would lighten your load. Sure, that could be as elaborate as hiring a private chef, but it could also be as simple as saying, Yes, thank you, to that friend or neighbor who asks if they can do anything. Maybe they'd be willing to make a pot of soup or pick up groceries for you. Outsourcing could also look like ordering groceries online or signing up for a meal kit or meal delivery service.

Focus on "better" instead of "perfect." I know how easy it is to compare ourselves to the highly curated social media feeds we're exposed to constantly, but just do yourself a favor and stop. Don't compare your real life to someone else's highlight reel. No single "perfect" diet exists. We are all so profoundly different, for one, but beyond that, what I've usually heard described as "perfect" actually just sounds super-restrictive and joyless. I truly believe you need to leave yourself room to live. If you want to eat more healthfully, make it about making "better" choices and let go of "perfect." Tune in to what feels great to *you*.

Not everybody goes here, but sometimes when it feels like there is so much out of your control, it's not uncommon to find yourself feeling a bit obsessive about things you can control. If you start to notice you're more consumed than usual by thoughts of food or are being especially harsh on yourself, reach out to a registered dietitian or licensed therapist for help. If time is an issue, consider finding someone who does telehealth sessions or using a resource like an app, which offer a range of services at varying price points to make care more accessible.

Choose your moments. Some years ago, I had a patient who transformed their health using a simple mantra: "Choose your moments." This helped them make mindful indulgences that allowed them to avoid feeling deprived while staying on track with healthy habits that supported their goals. Enjoy your favorite foods, but focus on making the decision to treat yourself and enjoy those foods as opposed to feeling like losing a tug of war.

No, you haven't "blown it." I hear this all the time: "I slipped up so I figured, what the hell—may as well eat the whole thing." (Or a version of that). Consider this a gentle reminder that you don't have to be "all or nothing" about healthy eating. This is why I'm a big fan of making room for intentional treats. If you do have an eating experience that goes differently than you would have liked, move on and remind yourself that you're human and also fully capable of getting right back on track with your next meal or snack.

CHAPTER 17

GET CURIOUS ABOUT
YOUR FOOD CRAVINGS

Suggested Listening: "(What's So Funny 'Bout)
Peace, Love, and Understanding?"
—NICK LOWE

Food cravings are one of the primary reasons I see people struggle to stay on track with healthy eating habits. They can feel overwhelming and intense, causing even more stress on top of whatever else someone might be going through. We're conditioned to think we should "conquer," "outsmart," or "curb" cravings with low-calorie approximations of off-limits indulgences, which is problematic—a total missed opportunity to understand what's behind those cravings. A 100-calorie pack of cookies doesn't offer much in the way of insight into your physical or emotional needs, you know?

I believe that cravings are the body's way of clueing us into our needs—mental or physical. I always encourage my patients to get curious rather than critical about cravings. How can we ever find peace with them if we refuse to explore them? Here are some things to know about food cravings.

Understand the Difference Between Physical and Emotional Cravings

A physical craving could be related to something short-term like a lack of sleep (when we're especially likely to crave carbs and sugar), an intense workout, menstruation, or not eating enough during the day. Other contributing factors may include pregnancy, underlying nutrient deficiencies, and chronic stress, all of which impacts our body's function. You might notice the craving feels like it comes out of nowhere or you can't get a particular flavor or texture out of your mind, even though it's not something you'd commonly think of.

An example I often use is women craving red meat during their period, a time when your iron stores are low because you're losing iron in your blood. Or if you have an underlying vitamin D deficiency, you may find salmon and eggs extra appealing. On an antibiotic and suddenly obsessed with sauerkraut or kimchi?

To share a personal example, when my insomnia was at its worst and my immune system was wrecked, I found myself craving wild sardines packed in olive oil. Up until that point in my life, I hadn't even been aware that I liked sardines in the first place, but suddenly I wanted them all the time. These tiny fish are rich in anti-inflammatory omega-3 fatty acids (which studies have shown help offset the effects of stress hormone cortisol[17]) and vitamin D, a key nutrient in immune system function.[18]

As I investigated further, the olive oil also made sense, given research tying the monounsaturated fatty acids and polyphenols in olive oil to decreased inflammation—help I certainly needed in that department.[19] This was around the time I was finishing up my fourth round of antibiotics, so I wasn't that shocked when I found myself eating kimchi and sauerkraut straight from the jar. Even though I was regularly taking my usual probiotic supplement, I couldn't seem to get enough fermented foods.

You don't have to have a nutrition degree to decode those physical cravings. If you're interested in unpacking why you might be craving a particular food, look up its nutrition information to find out if there's something in it that you may be lacking in.

Since I know that cravings for sardines are pretty weird, let's take a look at a much more common example: cravings for salty foods when you're stressed out. Your adrenal glands, which play a big role in the body's physiological stress response by releasing cortisol, sit above the kidneys.[20] Researchers have speculated that this could stimulate the kidneys, which are involved in our body's natural filtration system and could influence cravings for salt as a signal to help restore the sodium-potassium balance in cells. Research has also suggested that higher sodium levels may send signals to limit cortisol production.[21]

Some clues that you might be experiencing an emotional craving are if you have memories or experiences connected to that food or look at it as something that brings you comfort or feels like a pick-me-up. An example I often share is ice cream, one of the most common comfort foods people turn to in times of stress. Ice cream is a food that many of us associate with happy, care-free times like summer days and celebrations, and with that in mind, it's not super mysterious to be craving it when you feel over-whelmed by adult responsibilities or are working through some-thing difficult.

Another big one: sugar. While this can be physiological (for example, craving sugar for quick energy when you're exhausted), it is very often an emotional craving people struggle a lot with. This can also go back deep. Do you remember being a kid and getting a lollipop at the doctor's office? Or after the dentist? Our local bank used to give lollipops out to kids. Candy was given out as a treat, prize, or as a bribe. From a very young age, we are conditioned to view sugar as a reward. While some people are able to move on from that, countless people struggle with looking beyond sugar when they want to treat themselves or acknowledge a job well done.

Emotional cravings, like physical cravings, aren't bad; they're learning opportunities. Ask yourself what emotion you are hoping to get from that food. From there, that gives you the option to respond by either allowing yourself to have and enjoy that food (I'm a big believer in having the real deal on occasion rather than a "light" or "reduced guilt" approximation), or you can dig a little deeper and ask yourself what nonfood things could help you feel at least closer to the way you want to feel.

Important Step: Identify the Craving. Get Specific.

I know I said this before, but seriously, what is this culturally accepted bullshit about trying to "combat" a craving? Give yourself permission to name what it is you're craving and then get curious about it. Is it the flavor? The texture? A way that food makes you feel? Use that information for clues. If you've suddenly got almond butter on the brain and are really jonesing for that creamy texture, could it be you're tired and craving a high-calorie food that will give you slow-burning energy? Or if you're thinking more about PB&J sandwiches you enjoyed as a kid, that could be a sign you're in need of some comfort or carefree fun, a yearning for things to feel simple.

Determine Whether It's a Physical or an Emotional Craving

A physical craving offers a good chance to look at your overall diet quality and note whether there are any gaps you should be paying attention to on the regular. For example, if you're struggling with sugar cravings because you get energy crashes in the afternoon, that could be a sign you'd benefit from having a protein-rich snack then rather than playing mental tug-of-war with the vending machine.

If it's an emotional craving, get really honest with yourself about what that emotion is. I understand that this is easier said than done sometimes, especially if we're so wrapped up in caring for someone else that the idea of tuning into what's going on in our own heart and mind feels like a luxury or like something we "shouldn't" be doing when we're not the one with "real problems." You probably don't need me to tell you this, but when we let our emotions bottle up inside, they tend to find a way out anyway—usually something messier than if we'd just let ourselves acknowledge it right off the bat. Sometimes what comes up will surprise you, but resist the urge to judge yourself.

Respond Calmly

If you feel discomfort around what you're craving and / or why, take a deep breath as your next step. Some of you reading this who don't struggle with cravings as much might be, like, "WTF, why so dramatic?" But those of you who find food cravings to be tremendously uncomfortable and scary because they make you feel out of control, this is for you.

If this concept of leaning into cravings to understand them rather trying to stomp them out is new to you, give yourself some grace and some space. Know that it can take practice, and that's okay. As you get more comfortable checking in with yourself and listening to what comes up rather than trying to shut it down, enjoy the power that comes from people to say, "Hm. I notice I really need this, so I'm going to have it" or "I tend to crave this food when I'm feeling *xyz*. Is there something besides that food that will help me feel better?" or "Yeah, I know this is an emotional craving, but I just want to enjoy this treat and I feel totally confident in my ability to just pick right up with my usual healthy habits. An overall well-balanced diet includes room for occasional indulgences, and this is worth it to me."

CHAPTER 18

HOW TO DEAL
WITH STRESS EATING

Suggested Listening: "Cure For Pain"
—MORPHINE

There are a few different ways to approach stress eating. I doubt this will surprise you, but I'm a big believer in the idea that, in order to successfully deal with stress eating, you have to acknowledge it. Something I've worked on with many patients over the years is not being ashamed to point out to themselves when they're stress eating (or about to) and hitting the "pause" button. That gives them the opportunity to say, "Okay, this might not feel so great after—what's something else I can do?" and to dig deeper and ask themselves, "What do I really need?"

Stress eating often stems way back to a learned behavior that needs to be unlearned. In many cultures, as children we're placated with sugar and other palatable treats. When we get to adulthood, it's not crazy to still want a version of that lollipop as a reward for going to the doctor's office.

Sometimes it's also a matter of needing to stay busy, or to have something to do that will distract us from something we'd rather avoid. Eating is one of the few socially acceptable situations that allow us to take a break. You take a lunch break, or you can't talk when your mouth is full. There is also that eating is a physical act, something to pass the time, something to do with your hands. When you're stuffing your face, you've got something occupying your senses beyond whatever emotions you may be feeling.

Get Clear on Why You Stress Eat

That old cliché about awareness being the first step is a cliché for a reason: understanding the root of the issue gives clues as to how to deal with it. So when you ask yourself why you stress eat, listen to that answer.

Notice Patterns

Pay attention to what your triggers are. For example, are there particular situations or people who set you off? Is there a particular day of the week or time of day you're most likely to stress eat? Are there specific foods, flavors, or textures you find yourself gravitating toward when stressed? Are there specific foods you find it impossible to be moderate with or that you become fixated on? Don't judge, just note.

Brainstorm a Few Potential Strategies

Using the information that you gathered when tuning in to triggers and patterns, start brainstorming solutions. For example, if you notice yourself unable to stop eating trail mix when you're in the waiting area before your loved one's appointments because eating gives your hands something to do, you could try doing an activity to give you something to focus on (knitting or crocheting, writing in a journal, playing a game on your phone, doing a crossword puzzle—whatever works!) or switch to a nut you have to shell or a fruit you have to peel. It may take a few tries to find something that works, so be patient with yourself.

Don't Be Afraid to Ask For Help

If you find yourself overwhelmed by stress eating to the point where it impairs your mental and physical health, please don't be afraid to ask for help. There are trained professionals available to help you establish a healthier pattern. Even just one or a few sessions with someone who can help you understand and respond to that need for comfort eating can make a world of difference.

What to Eat When You're Stress Eating

This may be controversial, but for some people, I do think it's okay to have a few options for times when stuffing your face seems inevitable. Here are a few that have worked well for my patients and clients over the years.

Oranges. They're portable and the fact that they have a peel and you eat them in sections automatically slows you down and gives your hands something to do. They're also rich in folate, a vitamin that plays a role in supporting stable levels of "pleasure chemical" dopamine. The vitamin C in fruits also functions as an antioxidant to help fight stress-induced cell damage. The fluid in oranges and other water-rich fruits and vegetables boost hydration and help you feel full.

Blueberries offer a good amount of filling fiber, with about four grams per cup. The anthocyanins that give them their beautiful blue color also happen to be powerful antioxidants, as is their vitamin C.

Popcorn is a high-fiber whole grain that's especially popular because you can eat a large volume for comparatively fewer calories. A three-cup serving of air-popped popcorn contains about one hundred calories and three grams each of protein and fiber. This is also a great one if you find crunchy foods cathartic. Depending on what you season it with, it can go sweet or savory too. It's also easy to find premade or can be a portable option if you make some ahead of time.

Freeze-dried vegetables make another satisfying yet nutritious option if you crave crunchy and salty foods like chips when you're stressed. Beet, carrot, and kale chips, for example, provide around 150 calories per (fairly large) serving and also provide a good amount of filling fiber. Look for a product that is just that—vegetable and salt.

Salad with lots of greens and raw veggies can be a convenient choice when you're having a day where your stomach feels like a bottomless pit of despair or you want foods that take a long time to eat. Because of the water content of lettuce, cucumbers, tomatoes, and the like, a salad can help you stay hydrated and full. Veggies also provide fiber. That salad can be as low- or high-calorie as you need, but if it's going to be a meal, make sure you've got some protein and healthy fat in there to make it filling. One of my favorite hacks for a vegetarian protein option if you're skeeved by grab-and-go chicken or don't like hardboiled eggs is a big scoop of hummus or a serving of crispy chickpeas or nuts. A side salad can be a good option for a snack or for when you need to break a meal into multiple parts because of your schedule. And yes, it's okay if the other part of that meal is a piece of pizza or a deli sandwich—balance, right?

Sliced vegetables make a great stand-in for (or addition to) chips or crackers when you want an easy way to boost your nutritional intake while keeping calories in a realistic place. Pair with hummus or guacamole, for healthy fats and additional fiber, or with salsa if you just want some flavor but aren't super hungry.

Pistachios you have to shell yourself can force you to slow down, so they can be a soothing option if you know your stress eating has a lot to do with that factor. They can also help you stay physically satisfied and energized, thanks to the combination they offer of protein, fat, and fiber.

Obviously, this list is just to give you a few ideas, but use it as a springboard to help you come up with a few things that work you.

CHAPTER 19

MINDFUL DRINKING

Suggested Listening: "Waltz About Whiskey"
—WATCHHOUSE

S taying properly hydrated, finding your sweet spot with caffeine, and being careful with alcohol.

Hydration is essential for optimal cell function. Your cells have a lot of work to do in order to keep you going—and they need water to do their job. When you're even mildly dehydrated, you may feel sluggish, irritable, and unfocused. You can also develop headaches or dizziness. Because water also plays a role in helping fiber take up space in the stomach, drinking enough can help you feel full when eating. It's also essential for digestion, as water helps keep things moving through the GI tract, and dehydration can contribute to constipation. It also plays a role in preventing kidney stones and urinary tract infections as well as in skin hydration.

There's no official recommendation for how much *water* you need, but most health experts recommend eight eight-ounce glasses per day, or sixty-four ounces, which is equivalent to a half-gallon, or about two liters. There are factors that can impact your needs, such as climate (you'll need more if you live somewhere hot, humid, or dry), activity level, underlying health conditions, pregnancy or lactation, use of certain medications like diuretics, and whether your diet is low in water-rich foods or high in caffeinated beverages.

I've often said to "hydrate like it's your side-hustle," but if that sounds like nails on a chalkboard because you're juggling a ton, let's try this instead: hydrate because it will help you feel better.

If you're having a hard time drinking enough water, understand what makes it challenging for you to get enough (dislike of water, not remembering to drink, wanting to avoid using the restroom), and then come up with a realistic plan to address that barrier. You can also incorporate lots of water-rich foods like soup, fruits and vegetables, and yogurt. This approach works well too if you're trying to limit trips to the restroom.

When it comes to caffeine, keep in mind that the recommended limit for generally healthy adults is 400 milligrams per day, but many find that less feels better. Excess caffeine can cause jitters, irritability, and gastrointestinal issues, and it can interfere with sleep patterns. It can also amp up anxiety. Because caffeine is a mild diuretic, it may contribute to dehydration as well. For reference, here's the approximate caffeine content per serving of several popular sources:

- drip coffee: 95–200 milligrams;
- espresso: 65–75 milligrams;
- matcha: 70 milligrams;
- green tea: 25–30 milligrams;
- black tea: 45–50 milligrams; and
- cola: 35–45 milligrams.

Be Smart with Alcohol

Alcohol can be especially tricky for caregivers. It's often marketed as a way to de-stress, but it can become an unhealthy coping strategy. There are obviously many factors that influence whether someone will develop a dependence on or abuse alcohol, but because of the physical and emotional stress of caring for someone, caregivers are at an increased risk.

I spoke with holistic psychiatrist Ellen Vora, MD, about this. Understanding the mechanisms at work, she explains, can be helpful in establishing a healthy relationship to it. "I think that it's important to understand why we reach for alcohol. It's an enormous industry with a powerful lobby telling us it's a good choice. It's been effectively marketed." On a biological level, it has an effect that we, as humans, find appealing in the moment. "It enhances GABA in our brain, a neurotransmitter that increases our sense of ease and helps us feel relaxed. Our brains see that rush of GABA," which primes us to want to reach for alcohol when we feel stressed. The problem with that, though, is that "our body is wired for survival, not relaxation, so to restore homeostasis, the brain starts to convert GABA to glutamate, which is stimulating and causes you to wake up feeling anxious and irritated. And it's a cumulative effect." So the more you overdrink, the worse it can make you feel.[22]

"There's also a psycho-spiritual effect," she adds. "Culturally, we've done ourselves a disservice and don't hold space around grief. It's no wonder we want to avoid thinking about it and feeling it. Alcohol is a good option when we want to be less present! It's what we have been conditioned to do."

She advises calling out that urge to numb out and then actually sitting with those uncomfortable feelings. "As a psychiatrist, I would argue that in these moments, we want to go in deeply and be with our grief and have a healthy grief response.

When we numb and avoid feeling something with alcohol, it doesn't go away. It transmutes and gets lodged deeper into the body and can become future problems. Grief hurts. Feel it now, instead of in a different form later, such as chronic headaches, digestive issues, or low back pain. It's generally best to feel the full depth of our grief and emotional pain in the moment that it arises."

There are a lot of reasons to limit alcohol, whether that be during a stressful time or just overall. Here are just a few:

- Those calories provide no nourishment (in fact, drinking alcohol depletes the body of nutrients), making them "empty" calories that can easily lead to weight gain when not accounted for in the context of your diet.
- It can mess with your blood sugar in various ways, depending on what type you drink and whether you mix it with anything.
- It may impair your thinking or make it more difficult for you to respond safely to an urgent situation and put you more at risk of making mistakes (such as medication mistakes) with the person you're caring for.
- It's a lot harder to deal with a stressful situation if you're hungover.
- Consuming even moderate amounts of alcohol has been associated with increased risk of diseases such as some cancers, liver failure, and obesity. Yes, it has been associated with cardiovascular benefits, but take into account your unique health history and concerns.
- Because alcohol alters your brain chemistry, it can impact your mood and anxiety levels. This may be felt at the time of drinking or the next day.

- Even a little bit of alcohol can disrupt your sleep cycles, causing you to fall asleep quickly, only to wake up in the middle of the night.
- Because alcohol lowers inhibitions, you are more at risk of making decisions (or saying things) you may later regret or—this comes up a lot for people who struggle with making healthy food choices—making it harder to stay on track with healthy eating habits.
- There is an increased risk of accident.
- Alcohol interacts with many medications, there can be serious risks. Check any medications you're on, even over-the-counter ones.

How Much Is Too Much?

General recommendations for the United States Department of Agriculture (USDA) and World Health Organization (WHO) are for men to limit alcoholic beverages to two drinks per day. For women it's one drink per day. In the US, there have been pushes to reduce that recommendation, but as of the writing of this book, they remain unchanged.

While we often hear about the heart health benefits of wine, we hear a lot less about the increased risk of certain health conditions. For example, alcohol is considered one of the most modifiable risk factors for cancer. According to the American Cancer Society, alcohol use can be attributed to six percent of all cancers, and specifically, it has been linked to cancer of the breast, colon and rectum, esophagus, liver, mouth, throat, and voice box, and very likely the stomach.[23]

With that in mind, for those who are being mindful of risk reduction, I'll often recommend having less than that "moderate" amount in the course of a regular week, if at all.

What Counts as a Drink?

One standard drink contains about 1 gram of pure alcohol. This translates to about 12 ounces of beer (less if it's higher than 5% alcohol), 5 ounces of wine (which is typically about 12% alcohol), or 1.5 ounces of a distilled spirit (about 40% alcohol). Note that mixed drinks with several types of spirits may contain more than one serving of alcohol, meaning one martini may be equivalent to having three drinks. Of course, a larger pour of any type of alcohol also factors in. An 8-ounce glass of wine is more like 1.5 drinks.

It's important to pay attention to how different types of alcohol affect you. Because our bodies are all unique, we may process things differently. When it comes to what is the "best" drink, I always recommend choosing what you love and will feel most satisfied with, as opposed to choosing something simply because it's the lowest in calories or "cleanest" or whatever is being offered. Choose your moments to indulge and make it a worthwhile experience you can savor.

Seeking Help for Alcohol Dependence

If you feel like you are struggling with alcohol, don't be afraid to reach out for help. There are a wide variety of resources available, whether that be in-person programs, working with a therapist, or calling a hotline for next steps.

INTERVIEW WITH ELVIS COSTELLO

Suggested Listening: "Welcome to The Working Week"
—ELVIS COSTELLO

I have always admired Mr. Costello's drive to explore new styles of music and his ability to write songs from others' perspectives and tell stories. Getting into his records when I was a quietly angsty young adult also taught me that one can write with both bite and sensitivity, depending on what the occasion calls for.

He and my dad worked very closely together for many years. As he said when we spoke for this project, "Your father was one of the funniest, most straightforward people I ever met in a barrel of snakes and weasels. Yes, we worked together, but I was proud to call him a friend."

I always enjoyed attending his shows and seeing the energy that went into the event. He was always very kind to me whenever I would pop my head into the greenroom with my dad before a show or wait around for the adults to be done with a post-show meet-and-greet. I am very grateful to have had the opportunity to speak with him about the experience of touring.

What are some of the physical health challenges of touring?
Sleep is the key. Before I was in music, I worked for six months in a noisy, factory-sized computer department. I was a shift worker and it seemed to adjust my internal clock not to expect much or regular sleep. Even today, the excitement of a show is not easily turned off. The mind turns things over while the emotion of the night still resonates. If you actually get to go home to your own bed or even a hotel room in the same town, after the show, there can be something like an "evening" routine in which you eventually slow down and go to sleep.

If that sleep pattern gets too out-of-synch with the clock you can find yourself sleeping into an afternoon without any intention to be lazy. This means less time to see your surroundings, get a swim or some other exercise, eat something sensible. It isn't ideal, but it's not as if it is dangerous or poisonous, like working in a mine—but it is, in many unseen ways, a physical job.

I always liked the nighttime when I was a kid, so I didn't need to go to bed early. When I did shift work with computers, that was a bit of an adjustment at first because I really had to work through the night. It retrained me. And then a few years later I was keeping erratic hours with not always the healthiest activities. When I started traveling in music, there was a certain fearlessness and recklessness to what you did to yourself and what you could withstand. Obviously, in time, discretion becomes the better part of valor.

The travel didn't really affect me that much, though. I got used to it. I can always find the energy to do the show, but it will affect the recovery. If you sing hard and drive through the night, your body isn't aligned with the activities of the day. It's a small thing, not something people could tell, but I'm aware of it and aware that the vocal recovery is harder.

When there are 150 miles to the next hotel, you probably tell yourself, "I'll stay up." Anything over a three-hour drive and you have no choice but to grab a few hours of broken sleep. You might be asleep, but it is neither restful nor restoring. So, then you arrive and wake up just long enough to check into another hotel, around the time the early risers are going off to their jobs.

You then try to get your hotel room as dark as possible; bulldog clips can be useful for keeping the curtains shut tight, some people carry tape to cover blinking LED displays. I turn off the air conditioning and try to catch a few more hours of sleep so you can deliver a show at the same level.

Often it isn't your overall energy that is in question—that seems to arrive on cue—but simple vocal fatigue that requires this rest. Your voice is going to be foggy at afternoon rehearsal because it feels like morning, and you might only just get yourself properly awake by showtime. Too many consecutive days and nights like this can feel like permanent twilight.

Silence isn't so much golden as essential. I try to use the phone as little as possible, as you pitch your voice differently to the handset than to a microphone. It's not good to sing defensively. You have to sing without fear, and you have to know when to stop.

What are some of the mental and emotional challenges?

Keeping a lot of music and words in your head requires some mental agility but thinking too hard when performing can be inhibiting and you can lose the feeling. I will sometimes meticulously plan a show in advance based on lyrical themes—incredibly intricate connections between songs like scenes in a movie or the chapters of a novel—and then I'll get on stage and just want to turn the guitar right up and yell my head off singing someone else's song.

If we had a bad show when I was young, I usually imagined it was because people didn't understand us. Now I am probably more critical of my own work and cannot bear the time away from home if we fall short of what I know we can do.

Emotionally, this job means you have to accept time and distance away from people you love. However, playing well requires trust and feeling for your cohorts. I have shared a stage with Pete Thomas and Steve Nieve for over forty years, and Davey Faragher for nearly twenty. That's a lot of miles and shared excitement and even some disappointments and catastrophes.

In 2018, I had to curtail a tour when I badly overestimated my ability to recover from a very fortuitous surgery to remove a malignancy that might have made me very sick. I suppose the medical advisory regarding going back to a "physical job" after four weeks did not take account of the debilitating nature of our performance, travel, and recovery patterns. It was a stupid miscalculation on my part but mortifying to find my energy leave me all at once in the middle of a show, but "nobody's human," as my friend from Elvis Presley's band used to say.

Unfortunately, later that summer, I had to respond to a major crisis to my mother's health and there were several months of stressful transatlantic travel back and forth while the situation remained very grave. When I returned to the stage in the autumn, I slept with the phone on my pillow every night, anticipating a summons back to England. I probably shouldn't have been on stage at all that year, as I had injured myself and was singing with considerable inhibition and anxiety, but I'm all healed now.

Is there anything you learned along the way that you have found helpful? Or are there certain practices that have made a difference for you?

Anyone glancing at me would know I am not a picture of health. That said, what I do most nights would kill a horse. I have a strange engine. No matter how much I warm up or prepare, I can sometimes doubt I'm going to get through the first ten minutes, and two hours later they are side stage, saying "Get the hook, this guy won't come off."

Steam is good, to clear the head. Don't ever use analgesic throat spray. A renowned British throat specialist once recommended one drop of dish soap dropped into a water spray that you might use to chase away greenfly. Everybody has their potion.

Pre-show is a combination of relaxing and then speeding yourself up to the pace of showtime. Some people like to take short naps but I don't like to let my voice get sleepy. I play a portable record player loudly in my dressing room because it is more fun to sing along with music than to practice scales.

Jumping up and down or running upstairs can help get you started, but it's also important to relax. Before I get dressed for the show, I like to lie on the floor, if it isn't too dirty or dusty, and just stretch out and forget my cares for a minute or two. Get your head and shoulders on the floor and breathe deeply. It's easy to forget to breathe.

Do you travel with a bag of essential items?

It's difficult; you can't get on planes with many liquids, but I have a bag that I keep things in, like eucalyptus potions that I swear by for steam inhalation. Some people like slippery elm bark, some people like certain kinds of black currant paste or certain types of tea. I'll pack my bag to go away on the tour and there will always be one book I'll pack at the bottom of the case. I'll go, "Yeah, I'll read that on this tour." Never comes out of the case. You know, I'll bring some very, very learned book and then I'll end up reading magazines in the airport.

What advice would you give your younger self about health and wellness while touring?

I'd probably tell myself, don't drink that, there will be more in the next town. I did drink very enthusiastically for a number of years, and the day was just the inconvenient bright time between nightclubs. I was extremely fortunate not to become dependent and simply lost the taste for it more than twenty-five years ago and don't miss it.

We all know what we shouldn't do, what we shouldn't swallow, who we shouldn't kiss, but when you are young it is possible, if not necessary, to forget these cautions or prohibitions for a while. Some of your best songs stagger out of the debris of your most idiotic mistakes. Eventually, you have enough experiences to stop experimenting on yourself as if you were a chemistry set and simply imagine what might otherwise kill you or break your heart.

Just as crime novelists are rarely charged with murder but can make you believe they know how to commit, it helps if you can appreciate a bad motive with a clear head and a clean conscience, and you probably won't miss those people who were never really your friends.

Other than this I'd be the most unreliable person to offer advice on anything.

What is something that would surprise most people about what it's like to be on tour?

That it is the longest of drum rolls for the shortest of tricks. Try imagining this trip might be your last and you may get the best out of it.

MOVEMENT

CHAPTER 20

WHY MOVEMENT MATTERS

Suggested Listening: "Swept Away"
—THE AVETT BROTHERS

P hysical activity has been well established as an effective stress management tool. It can help improve energy and mood and has even been shown to help lessen perceived stress.[24] For those who struggle with weight management during times of stress, exercise can play a supportive role when combined with a healthy diet. It also helps our nervous system adapt and helps maintain good immune function.[25]

More and more I find myself using the term "movement" instead of "exercise" or "physical activity" because it seems so much more inclusive. Pretty much any resource for caregivers will tell you that exercise is beneficial, but in practice I've found that sometimes calling it "exercise" can be intimidating for someone who's juggling a lot and is working with way less time and energy. We tend to associate "exercise" with trips to the gym, going for runs, playing sports, or taking a group class—all things that sound time-consuming or daunting. I like that "movement" can include so many different kinds of things, structured or not, and has a sense of ease and flexibility about it. While I will use all three of these terms throughout these chapters, I felt it was important to explain that.

Movement was an especially important part of my own self-care routine when my dad was sick. I look back and acknowledge that I had the luxury of being single, childless, mostly self-employed, and splitting caregiver duties with my mother and sister, but even with all that flexibility, I remember having to be intentional about making it a regular part of my routine. Though I felt guilty sometimes for carving out that time, I would remind myself of what I tell my patients: taking care of yourself helps you take better care of others. Also: even a little bit counts.

A few of the biggest mental and physical benefits to caregivers I like to highlight are:

- stress management;
- improved sleep;
- boosting self-esteem;
- promoting better energy and stamina;
- improved cognitive function;
- supporting a healthy immune system;
- reduced risk of adverse health conditions; and
- assistance with weight management.

That said, if you're struggling with making movement a part of your life, here are some of the tips and tools that have been most helpful with my patients and clients over the years.

Ditch the "All or Nothing" Mindset

Where I see many people struggle with physical activity relates to that "all or nothing" mentality with which so many approach exercise. Those who may be used to vigorous long runs or the hour-long group classes may feel like shorter or less intense work-outs aren't "worth it" or that they don't count.

This is usually where I put on my health coach hat and say, "Something is better than nothing." Because it is! Ever notice how, if you're feeling frazzled and get up and walk around even for five or ten minutes, you usually feel better after? Every time you move your body, give yourself a mental high five and acknowledge that you did something nice for yourself. You can even note the specific benefit that resonates most with you.

Another favorite tip that has worked for my patients and that I've used in my own life is to exercise in shorter bursts through the day. Several five, ten, and/or fifteen-minute sessions where you move with intention can help you feel great. For example, maybe you do a few minutes of ab exercises and a few push-ups in the morning when you first get up, then take a fifteen-minute walk in the afternoon, and then in the evening you do some stretches before bed. If it helps you to have a plan (however loose or struc-tured serves you) that can help you know what to do when you have those little windows of time so you don't spend it messing around on your phone. I'm a big fan of utilizing apps or making a Pinterest board to track your favorite online resources or keeping a list either on your phone or in a place you will regularly see it.

I spoke with Lauren Chiarello Mika, who is a two-time cancer survivor and mom to twin boys. She's also a fitness professional and cancer exercise trainer. I got to know her through a mutual friend when we were all still living in New York. Beyond being a great teacher with an infectious positive energy, she has an incredible way of bringing people together for meaningful causes. I always came away from her fundraising events with a smile on my face and having met at least a couple people doing incred-ible things to help make the world a better place. From having been through cancer treatment herself and also from navigating the experience of having one of her sons being hospitalized for the first few months of his life, including a surgery to rule out a liver disease, she has a unique perspective.

"It's a marathon, not a sprint," she says. "For caregivers, I would say that self-care is responsible. It's crucial to staying resilient. Practicing gratitude is a pillar of resilience—write it down, talk about it with your significant other, and look for a moment of joy in each day."

"The biggest piece," she says, "is flexibility and an open mind." She also is a fan of the phrase "done is better than perfect" and applies that to movement practices, especially during times of stress. "We may have this ideal vision of our exercise routine" or how it was for us in the past. Getting caught up in comparing the past to our current reality can feel frustrating. What can help, she says, is "understanding that we go through phases of life and that some are going to be more challenging than others—there are difficult times and there are joyful times—and accept that and meet yourself where you are."

She points out that acknowledging even small positive shifts we experience in our energy can be motivating and help us feel better about moving less. "If I'm a three and then do ten minutes of yoga and I'm a five or a six after, that's still an improvement." Let go of perfection, she says, and "do the best you can in this moment and focus on how you'll feel after."

Don't Compare

Another trap I see a lot of folks fall into: comparing themselves to others or to their past selves when they did not have as much on their plate. And yes, I know this is an extremely easy hole to fall into, especially with social media constantly feeding us specific imagery of what "healthy" looks like. We need to be mindful of what we internalize and to take steps to remind ourselves that everyone is on their own journey and that what we see is highly curated. People post what they want you to see.

Stop following social media accounts that trigger comparisons and instead, fill your feed with things that make you feel good. For me, that's cute animals doing cute things. For you, it might be pretty flowers, or funny memes, or laughing babies—I don't know. There's something for everyone.

Of course, the comparison game takes place in real life too. I know we all have that friend or acquaintance who always likes to brag or post about how many miles they ran that day or how hard they worked out, or maybe it's that weirdly competitive person at your gym or in a workout class who makes comments about others' performance or appearance? Or both. Pay attention to how certain people and environments affect your mental and physical energy. This could be a good time to find a way to get some distance from those people and seek out settings and / or people that help you feel energized. Give yourself permission to change your routine and let stuff go.

It's also totally normal to get sucked into comparing yourself where you are now to where you were at a different time in your life. Practice self-compassion by paying attention to how you talk to yourself and reframing negative thoughts. For example, if you find yourself lamenting going for a shorter run than you used to go for or for not being able to lift as heavy weights as you may have been used to in the past, try expressing appreciation for being able to do any movement to take care of your brain and body right now. If it helps, list off what you've been doing and how it feels good. Shift to celebrating and acknowledging your resilience and how you are learning to be flexible. If you have a journaling practice or make mental gratitude lists, acknowledge your efforts.

Chiarello says, "Drown out the noise—it's accessible twenty-four/seven. Disconnect and focus on what makes *you* feel good.

Try things that make you feel energized and have some self-compassion. We can try to reframe and rewire our brains with more positive messaging about ourselves."

When Movement Becomes Escapism

This is less common, but for some, movement can become escapism. I spoke with Whitney Tucker, a hormone coach and mindset mentor, founder of Embodied Potential© and Sync to Thrive© who supports women through hormonal literacy, mindset approaches, and physical wellness practices. I first met Whitney when Athleta put us together for a yoga and nutrition workshop where she led the group through a yoga flow and I gave a talk about diet. Since then, we have collaborated on a number of classes and programs geared toward helping people feel calmer, stronger, and more balanced in their physical and mental health.

When I interviewed her about movement for caregivers, something she said really spoke to me. "I think movement can be therapeutic but also escapism. If done without consciousness and awareness of emotions, it can keep a person from processing and expressing emotions."

I flashed back to the physical therapy sessions I had to squeeze in early into my dad's illness. It had started when an old sports injury came back to haunt me over the summer because I had been rushing around town and back and forth between New Jersey and the city, lugging heavy bags and not wearing the right shoes. I was so fixated on getting to where I had to be, I was tuned out of the signals my body was sending me. I was also doing too much yoga because taking classes where I followed an instructor's cues gave me a break from my own thoughts. But then one October morning in the Port Authority concourse near the 7 train, in the tunnel that connects the 1/2/3, A/C/E, and 7 lines with the bus terminal, I felt the familiar twinge in my hamstring and knew I couldn't ignore it anymore. A few weeks later, I felt the lipoma in my lower back (another "tell" when I have been moving without mindfulness) and knew I was doing the Overuse Injury Dance again.

"For people who have habitually used movement to escape," said Tucker, "they probably should sit and meditate" and work on allowing themselves to actually process the emotions they're feeling first. "As long as it's an honoring and acceptance of the emotion, movement can shift you," in a positive way, but using it to numb yourself from feeling what you're feeling can backfire. "Some people really exhaust themselves and can get addicted to it." She adds that because strenuous workouts are a form of stress (if good stress), when we don't allow time for recovery, it can wear you out and overtax your endocrine system, potentially lead to injury, and may even make it harder for you to cope. Build in time for rest.

A few early warning signs to watch out for are feeling physically run down or like you're not recovering well from workouts or noticing that you beat up on yourself or get into an overly negative headspace when you don't get any movement. Don't be afraid to seek out the help of a recovery specialist if you suspect you're overdoing it.

CHAPTER 21

MAKING TIME VERSUS HAVING TIME

Suggested Listening: "And Your Bird Can Sing" (Take 2) /
Anthology 2 Version
—THE BEATLES

Have you ever noticed that there are certain things that, no matter how busy you are, you always seem to be able to find time for? And on the flip side, are there other things it can feel darn near impossible to get around to?

I used to think about this a lot when I was dating. More than once I told someone, "If this were meant to be a thing, it wouldn't be so hard to actually find time to get together." Of course, this can also come up with friendships, work and social obligations, and yes, with self-care practices. Some may feel like a natural part of your life, and others make you just want to throw your hands up and say, "I just don't have time."

This can apply to movement as well: It's not about *having* time—it's about *making* time.

Get Motivated to Move

Motivation is a vital piece of the picture. Sure, you can have a great plan, but if you can't bring yourself to follow it, you're not going to reap the benefits. I one-hundred-percent understand how challenging it can be to get motivated to do something when you feel like you're pressed for time or when you feel like you have to be constantly available and can't really plan ahead. Or maybe you're just exhausted and struggling to find the right balance between rest and activity.

Remember that saying, "an object at rest remains at rest?" A lot of it is about overcoming inertia when it comes to making it happen. If you are adequately rested but you're still struggling with getting or staying motivated to move, don't beat up on yourself. Take a breath and try these tips to get you going.

First things first, check in with yourself (and be honest) about whether movement or rest will serve you best in that moment. If the answer is "movement," try whichever of the following resonate with you:

- Remind yourself of the benefits. Sometimes reconnecting with your "why" can make a huge difference in getting you to lace up your sneakers or unroll your yoga mat.
- Think of how great you'll feel when you're done.
- Tell yourself you only have to do five minutes.
- Remind yourself that even a little bit counts.
- Incentivize it. If knowing you can treat yourself to a (nonfood) reward will get you moving, go for it. It can be something tangible, like buying yourself something you want if you work out a certain number of days you've set as your goal (as an example) or catching up on a favorite show or reading a trashy novel while you walk on a treadmill or ride a stationary bike.
- Reframe it as something you're doing to take care of your own mental and physical health, which helps you be a better caregiver.

CHAPTER 22

MAKING THE MOST
OF LIMITED TIME

Suggested Listening: "Rise"
—EDDIE VEDDER

Short on time? No worries! There are lots of ways to be active even if you're just squeezing it into a tiny amount of time. Always acknowledge your efforts and take the time to appreciate yourself.

When choosing which type of movement to do, says Tucker, a lot depends on what your goals are. Think of the outcome you want and which activities will lead to that outcome. While she encourages setting up a plan for specific goals you have, on those days you need to be flexible, as long as you get moving, she says, it doesn't matter so much what that looks like. "What movement do you find joy in? What do you intuitively like doing? What habit formation works for you? Do you need a lot of incentive? Are you driven by rewards? Do you need accountability? Are you social and maybe need a friend to go on walks with? What satisfies us in movement is unique to each person's personality. It should be treated as an investigation and will likely change as the foci of your goals and commitments do."

If shorter bursts of activity work for you, think about what you want to get out of those bursts. Do you want to get your heart rate up? Build muscle? Blow off some steam? Unwind?

"While getting on the treadmill for twenty minutes and watching terrible news on TV may be better than nothing," says Tucker, "maybe meditation or breath work would serve you better." And what serves you best might be different on different days. The goal, says Tucker, is to "do something with your body and get into flow state, where you're moving with present-mind intention and not thinking about what's going to happen later and what happened before." She also encourages mixing up what you do to offer the brain and body some variety. For example, maybe you try a new route or a new activity, or maybe you choose from a toolbox of activities you know you enjoy and get value from.

If You Have Five to Fifteen Minutes

Chiarello says, "If someone has even five to fifteen minutes, a short pocket of time, I think we're so quick to grab the phone or hop on the computer. It can be so easy to say, 'I'll do this after I check a few emails' but all that will still be waiting. Set it to the side and can we get five, ten, fifteen minutes in and then go back to those emails. I like to stretch (neck rolls, arm circles, bring my hands to my shoulders). We hold a lot of tension in the neck and shoulders. When you are on your computer or device, think about your posture. Also, think about core exercises. It improves posture, reduces tension, and can help you breathe better.

"I would say stretch and core exercises will go a long way, and you don't need to take a lot of time. If you have just a short pocket of time and maybe can't even change your outfit, these are mindful movements that are quick, effective, and give you the most bang for your buck. It's about your mental focus. We really have to shift away from our devices. They're addictive, and it's a practice to get off of them."

If You Have Thirty Minutes

If you have thirty minutes, you may wish to do a more structured class or workout. If you find it easier to have something to follow, an on-demand video workout that you can do in the comfort of your home can be a great way to enjoy a taste of a live class but in a more convenient way. If you're craving something quieter or more meditative, a thirty-minute walk or bike ride may feel invigorating and restorative.

Moving Through Your Emotions

Different types of movement may help us deal with different emotions. An important step is to first give yourself a chance to process what you're feeling physically and emotionally. It's also totally normal, by the way, to experience a physical response to emotions: think crying, shaking, clamping your fists, gritting your teeth, feeling frozen in place—these are all ways your body reacts. Think about animals, and how they growl or quiver or run away; fight, flight, or freeze. We have those impulses too.

Building awareness of what and how you feel is a valuable tool you can develop, so this processing can help prevent those emotions from being stored in the body and coming back to haunt us later. If you're not used to giving yourself that space to become aware of what you're feeling in the moment (those of you who cope by "just pushing through," I'm talking to you), this may take some practice and be scary as hell. If you feel overwhelmed, consider working with a therapist or talking to someone you trust who can offer support.

When it comes to incorporating movement to help you shift through uncomfortable emotions, Tucker recommends focusing on what can help you transition back to a neutral state from that fight, flight, or freeze. Pay attention to what it feels like your body wants to do. While every person is different in terms of which types of movement will help them through which emotions, here are some examples.

When you feel anxious or scared: Tucker recommends slow breath work or calming yoga postures to help with feelings of anxiety or fear. "I will go into plow position because, if my knees can rest at my ears and I can't hear, I'm taking out visual and auditory stimuli. Or I'll get into child's pose or a restorative pose where I also have less stimuli."

When you feel angry or frustrated: "If I recognize that I have anger," says Tucker, "I usually do something with high intensity like running, jumping rope, or boxing." It can feel great to sweat out what is stressing you out or causing you pain and it releases some endorphins.

When you're exhausted: It's important to consider whether you're tired just that particular day or whether you feel like exhaustion has become your new normal. "If it's a one-off thing," says Tucker, "you might really just need rest." However, if you're exhausted all the time, she recommends trying short bursts of moderate intensity cardio (instead of steady state cardio) or activities like walking and gentle yoga. "If I have a client I see a few times a week who comes and says they're tired, sometimes I'm, like, 'Let's breathe. Let's put you in a restorative posture and get your endocrine system working properly.' Sometimes people just need to sleep and they won't give themselves permission."

If you're struggling with the idea of rest, take a moment to think about your programming. Culturally, there is massive pressure to always be producing, and this implication that taking a break (aka to rest) is "not producing" and therefore a bad thing. This can be especially tricky for caregivers who are also balancing a job or other responsibilities where they feel like they need to always be doing something or keeping up.

Tucker calls bullshit. "This idea that if we're resting we're not producing . . . that's counterproductive." She works a lot with premenopausal women and helps them go with the flow of their menstrual cycle. "If we don't regard our innate biological rhythms, we're signaling to our endocrine system that we're not listening to it. Sometimes you're going to have weeks where you'll feel like, 'I can do double,' and some weeks where you can do half—especially for pre-menopausal women, is dictated naturally by their hormones—and it's all valid."

INTERVIEW WITH
SARAH LEE GUTHRIE

Suggested Listening: "Coming into Los Angeles"

—SARAH LEE GUTHRIE

Third generation singer-songwriter Sarah Lee Guthrie is a touring recording artist to whom I was introduced by Billy Keane—you'll hear from him later in the book. Essentially growing up on the road with her father Arlo Guthrie, she worked as his road manager in the late 1990s before turning to performing herself. She has a unique perspective that led her to focus on staying well in order to keep up with the pace of touring.

What are some of the physical health challenges of touring?
Finding really good food is one of the most challenging aspects. Getting good rest is hard too. You're moving. Making sure to pace yourself is the thing. Especially in the early days I'd go hardcore, full-on, and two weeks into the tour I'd get sick.

I have had pretty much every level of experience, from being by myself in a car, sleeping in parking lots and on people's couches, to being with my ex-husband and family in a van. That was most of my career. And then, every once in a while, I've had the ability to be on the tour bus with my father. The bus being absolutely the best-case scenario, where the bus has a kitchen and a refrigerator, and the venue has catering. That makes it easier to stay healthier and be in a good place.

Performing takes a lot out of you physically. It doesn't matter if there are five or five thousand people in the audience. If you're performing to the best of your ability, you're giving 150 percent of yourself. Even though the adrenaline keeps you energized, often-times, you're exhausted. When you're able to tour on the bus, you can actually catch up and keep up with your needs. Some days, I will sleep all day, go to soundcheck, go back to bed, and then get up to go to the show. When I don't have to do the merch and sound and set-up myself, that's the ideal way. When you're in a van and doing everything yourself plus raising a couple of kids, that can take it out of you. You always get sick after the tour. The adrenaline drops and you can feel your own body and you realize how worn out you are.

What are some of the mental and emotional challenges?

For me, it's the transition that's hard. I believe it really takes an entirely different nervous system to be on the road and performing night after night than it does to be home. It's equally challenging to be getting on the road. It takes me four to five days to get that nervous system developed to go-go-go. After COVID, I had been home for eight months, the longest in my life, and when I got back on the road, it took me a while. I felt shakier and it took me a while to go from being a homebody to being on the road again.

Many people I've taken on the road, who thought they wanted to do this (like nannies or friends), three days in they wanted to go home because they couldn't take not knowing where they were going to get their next meal or when they could get some sleep. A normal nervous system doesn't do that. I grew up on the road, so

I know this quite well. When I get into it and face those fears it's fine, and once I get into the tour it becomes easier.

Then when you get home and have to deal with simple household things like dishes you don't have to do on the road (I still have to do laundry on the road!) is sometimes really overwhelming. When I get home, I also find I let down and let out and open myself up to more energies. When I'm on the road, I'm more protected, energetically. For me, when I'm home, I can't believe that I do that and get up on the stage and sing in front of all those people! It's crazy! It feels like two different people. Then when I'm on the road I can't imagine staying in one place.

What advice would you give to artists about health and wellness while touring? Or is there anything you wish you had known when you were just starting out?

In terms of keeping good health, I think that pace is the most important. I think a lot of kids who are on tour and have, like, eighteen shows in a row, that wears you down. I believe in rest and balance. In order to give your best performance, you have to take some downtime. I meditate a lot and make sure to find a quiet place. I think that that really adds to my ability to perform well. If you can find those moments to walk away from your band and your friends in the towns you visit who want to see you, you just have to say no sometimes. For me, it has to do with slowing down and self-care, taking those moments.

What is something that would surprise most people or that people get wrong about life on the road?

I always get, "Oh my gosh, you get to see all these beautiful places!" when really, we end up pulling into town into a dirty alley that smells like trash. You go into the venue and, depending on where you're playing, most of the time you don't see the city at all, and you don't have the chance to enjoy the best restaurants and the sights. It's not a tourist experience. Even though I've been to thousands of cities, I don't know them. It's hotels and venues and parking lots. It is, to me, wonderful, but if you're just a regular person wanting to experience these towns, that ain't it.

When you're on the road, do you carry a bag of essentials? If so, what's in there?

In order to stay well, I am Remedy Girl. You're out amongst all these people, and your nervous system and immune system are taxed. You're under stress whether you feel it or not. I use Emergen-C packets. I also keep oil of oregano with me at all times. I use apple cider vinegar daily. I use slippery elm for my throat if it's overworked. I definitely take honey and bourbon. Gargling with salt water is also so healing to the vocal cords.

I also use essential oils like lavender. It's simple but incredibly powerful, especially if you have a little anxiety before a show or can't sleep after. I also use sandalwood and frankincense. Both have that high vibration and spiritual power. If I'm in my head too much and need to wipe that clear and remind myself I'm here to serve and it's not about me, I use them to resolve that mind activity so I can get out of the way and be that vessel I'm supposed to be and get into the right headspace before a show. If I'm tired or have some congestion, I have a blend called Olbas, and that is amazing. It's a mix of mints and some other ingredients. I put it on my palm and breathe it in or on the back of my neck and it energizes me and clears out my sinuses. It's great for clearing the air in hotel rooms too. I will take a wet washcloth, pour the Olbas on it, and lay it over the air conditioning.

Vitamin D3 and iodine are two other things. A lot of people don't realize how important it is to take care of your adrenals and immune system.

None of these things work, though, unless you're in tune with your body and realize your immune system is low in the first place. If you're in it for the long haul, partying is a hard thing to keep up. You don't have a good sense of where your body is.

SLEEP

CHAPTER 23

THE SLEEP STRUGGLE

Suggested Listening: "Head Underwater"
—JENNY LEWIS

As I shared earlier, sleep was my biggest self-care struggle throughout my dad's illness. The second I'd lay down at night, my eyes would pop open. And forget turning off the light—it was like the second the lamp went out something lit up bright and hot in my head.

I felt like such a fraud. By day I was helping others with their health and wellness—and celebrating the success they got from following my tips—but I couldn't get a handle on this one key element of wellness in my own life. Nice one, universe. I recognized that these were special circumstances, but it was so frustrating.

Looking back, I wonder if I had known then what I know now about sleep hygiene, would it have worked for me? My sleep routine at the time consisted of a quick shower, magnesium powder in warm water if I remembered, and using my bedside light bulb as a makeshift diffuser by tipping a few drops of lavender essential oil onto it like my mother had taught me to do when I went off to college, a time when I'd had terrible insomnia. I sometimes popped a Benadryl when it got really bad. I was always journaling.

It was actually this experience that inspired me to get really serious about sleep hygiene. I wish I could tell you that since then, I've had zero struggles with sleep. The annoying truth, of course, is that, yes, you can be doing everything right and will still occasionally find yourself wide awake at three in the morning with your mind racing. The key thing to note is how frequently that happens. If it's a few times a year, okay, maybe you're good, but if it's happening at least once every week or more than a few times a month, or you get into a bad cycle and can't seem to get back on track, it's worth looking into.

I acknowledge that as a caregiver, you're dealing with a bigger workload and likely a big-ass emotional load, but that doesn't mean you have to suffer. Establishing a healthy sleep routine and having a list of things to do if you wake up in the night can make a significant difference in helping you have better sleep more often.

Why Does Sleep Matter?

An occasional poor night of sleep (though unpleasant) won't make a huge long-term difference, but when you're consistently sleep deprived, it can lead to serious health issues.[26]

Some common signs of sleep deprivation are:

- fatigue;
- impaired cognitive function (including decision-making);
- mood changes (for example, feeling more stressed, anxious, irritable);
- reduced attention span; and
- worsened memory.

Long-term consequences of chronic sleep deprivation may include:

- cardiovascular disease;
- diabetes;
- hormonal imbalances;
- impaired immune system function;
- mental health disorders such as anxiety, depression, and bipolar disorder;
- obesity; and
- pain.

I know that dwelling on these health risks in the wee hours can add to stress you have around not sleeping, so be kind to yourself. Take a moment to acknowledge what you're going through and then come up with a better plan than "All the coffee."

What I share in these pages may be a good start, but if you need more, don't be afraid to reach out to your doctor to help you come up with a plan designed to suit your individual needs.

CHAPTER 24

SET THE STAGE
FOR QUALITY SLEEP

Suggested Listening: "Even the Darkness has Arms"
—BARR BROTHERS

Taking steps to optimize our sleep environment and establish a sleep schedule can help promote good sleep. Here are a few steps you can take to set the stage for quality rest.

Make Sleep a Priority

If you don't prioritize your sleep, no one will. If you're not used to being intentional about it, start with small steps. Take an honest look at whether you are blocking out enough time for rest. As a caregiver juggling many responsibilities, I understand if this idea seems a little laughable, but if you're finding that you're often staying up too late doing things that aren't essential (hello, social media scrolling or binge-watching shows) or taking on extra tasks you could just say "no" to or outsource, it might be time to draw a few boundaries. Another way a need to prioritize sleep may show up is if you have an uncomfortable bed or bedroom or have been putting off getting shades or have fixable disruptions you haven't dealt with, it may be time to make the changes you need.

Here are some tips to help you optimize your sleep:[27]

Stick to a Schedule. Go to bed and wake up around the same time each day—even on the weekends.

Set Boundaries. Yes, this means putting a cap on responding to emails or scrolling on social media. Set realistic expectations around when you will be unavailable. Of course, this may still mean that you need to be available to the person you're caring for. Everyone else, though? They can wait. If you're feeling guilty about this, remind yourself that you're a better caregiver when you're well-rested.

Resist Long Naps. This can mess with your sleep cycle in a big way by making it harder to fall asleep at night. If you really need a quick refresh, keep it to about thirty minutes.

Cultivate a Sleep Routine. Consistently doing a few things to prepare for bed can help signal to the brain and body that it's time to call it a night. For example, this may be putting on pajamas, brushing your teeth, and enjoying a quiet activity that helps you relax. You can keep it super simple or add extra elements like a shower, stretching, meditating, or using aromatherapy. Because blue light from electronics can disrupt our circadian rhythm, resist the urge to drift off watching TV, or at least consider buying a pair of blue light blocking glasses. If you have trouble making time, set a bedtime alarm on your phone.

Optimize Your Sleep Environment

- Keep the room cool. Research has shown that around sixty-five degrees Fahrenheit is an optimal temperature for sleep.
- Keep the room dark. Exposure to light can reduce

levels of melatonin, a hormone that regulates our circadian rhythm. Consider investing in blackout curtains or wearing an eye mask. Avoid watching television in bed and cover blinking lights from electronics.

- Don't keep your phone by the bed. I know this one is hard, but it's powerful. If you're anxious about missing a text message or call from the person you're caring for, at least keep it out of immediate reach and set the few people or places you do want to be able to reach you as favorites in your phone.
- Reserve your bed only for sleeping and sex.
- Your mattress, pillows, and bedding can make a difference. You want to feel supported and comfortable. If you find yourself constantly needing to readjust, consider exploring other options that may be a better fit.
- Aromatherapy can be useful in promoting restful sleep. Research has shown that lavender can be especially helpful.

Avoid Things that Disrupt Sleep

- caffeine;
- alcohol;
- heavy, late meals;
- electronics within an hour of going to bed (laptops, computers, tablets); and
- trying to squeeze in work right before bed, amping up your "to-do list" brain.

Eat Foods to Support Restful Sleep

Certain compounds and nutrients have been shown to play a role in promoting restful sleep. Here are the main ones:

Melatonin. This hormone helps regulate our circadian rhythm and sleep cycle. Levels rise in response to darkness and decrease with light exposure. Supplements are the most common way people boost their levels when needed, but you can find it in a few foods such as eggs, tart cherries and tart cherry juice, milk, fish, and nuts.[28]

Serotonin. This mood-regulating neurotransmitter is also involved in our sleep cycle because it can help us settle down and drift off. It also plays a role in melatonin production. Eating foods that enhance serotonin production have been shown to help improve sleep and mood.

Tryptophan. This amino acid is a precursor to serotonin. When consumed through food, it's converted into 5-Hydroxytryptophan (5-HTP), which is then used by the body to make serotonin and melatonin.[29] You can find tryptophan in animal proteins like meat, poultry, fish, eggs, and dairy, but there are some plant sources available too, such as oats, chickpeas, and honey. Supplements of 5-HTP are also available.[30]

Calcium. This mineral plays many roles in the body (we usually hear about it in relation to bone health) but the way in which it impacts sleep is that it helps regulate our muscle movements and blood pressure to help us calm down and settle into sleep. Calcium is also involved in cell signaling and impacts how the body utilizes tryptophan. Find it in dairy products as well as in smaller amounts in leafy greens, tofu, white beans, and canned salmon.[31]

Vitamin B6. This water-soluble vitamin aids in the production of melatonin and serotonin. It's found in many foods, including bananas, beans, chicken, fish, and whole grains, just to name a few sources.[32]

Potassium. This mineral is also involved in muscle and nerve function. In addition, it can help soothe muscle aches and nighttime twitches so you can drift off more comfortably. Find it in avocado, banana, dairy products, oranges, leafy greens, potatoes, tomatoes, and winter squash like pumpkin and butternut squash.[33]

Magnesium. Another mineral that helps regulate the function of our nerves and muscles, magnesium also assists in regulating blood pressure and blood sugar. It's also thought to counteract stress hormone cortisol. Some good food sources include bananas, chicken, dairy products, fish, nuts, and spinach.[34]

Carbohydrates. Carbs can be your friend when it comes to restful sleep. Eating carbohydrates enhances tryptophan levels in the blood by causing an insulin release that then promotes absorption of amino acids, including tryptophan. The type of carbs matters, though. Reach for complex carbs like whole grains, beans, fruit, and starchy vegetables like sweet potatoes—they'll break down more slowly than refined carbs and keep your blood sugar stable so you don't wake up starving in the middle of the night.

What About Sleep Supplements?

There are lots of sleep supplements on the market promising to help you sleep better. A few of the most common ones you'll see are melatonin, magnesium, valerian root, and lavender, to name a few. Very often, they are sold as a blend. I discuss some of these with my patients to help them make an informed decision but always recommend talking to your doctor about potential concerns like interaction with medications, potential adverse reactions, proper dosage, and the like. We're all different and have different things we're dealing with, so what works for one person may be different from what will benefit someone else.

Strategic Napping

Using naps as a strategic part of your wellness routine when you're in a caregiver role can help you feel better rested if you're struggling with poor or interrupted sleep and experience unexpected fatigue. Naps have been associated with:

- improved alertness and cognitive function;
- improved mood;
- reducing fatigue; and
- relaxation.

If you find yourself needing to nap daily, it wouldn't be a bad idea to talk to your doctor about what might be contributing to your fatigue and what longer term solutions might be helpful. In the short term, however, here are a few tips for napping.

Keep it short. The longer you nap, the more likely it is you'll be groggy upon waking. Aim to nap for ten to twenty minutes.

Avoid napping after 3:00 pm. When you nap too close to evening, it can interfere with your sleep cycle.

Optimize your sleep environment. Same as you would when going to bed for the night, when settling in for a nap, you want to make sure your sleeping area is as restful as possible. Keep it cool and dark and limit distractions like electronics.[35]

CHAPTER 25

WHAT TO DO WHEN YOU CAN'T SLEEP

Suggested Listening: "The Sound of Silence"
—SIMON & GARFUNKEL

I t happens to all of us sometimes, but when being up in the middle of the night starts to feel like the norm, it can take a serious toll on your mental and physical health. Having some tools to choose from in those frustrating sleepless moments can be comforting in and of itself. Try as few or as many as you like. Over time, you'll get a sense of which ones serve you best. Here are some of my favorites that my clients and patients and I have found helpful:

Meditate. If you suffer from an overactive nighttime mind, meditation can be helpful. There are so many meditation methods out there, so see what works for you. Some people prefer guided meditations, whereas others prefer to put on soothing sounds or to sit in pure silence. You can be sitting up, lying down—whatever makes you feel most relaxed. Instead of pressuring yourself to empty your mind, see if you can make it about quieting the chatter or clearing clutter from your mind. You wouldn't expect a room you live in not to have any furniture in it, but think of the difference between having lots of crap on the floor and clothes hanging out of drawers and closet doors wide open as opposed to how much better it feels when there's space to move and things are tucked away neatly.

Journal. If you find yourself in an anxiety loop with thoughts swirling like crazy or to-do-list brain on full volume, write that stuff down. This can help disrupt that cycle and quiet the noise. You might find that getting your thoughts out of your head and onto paper to be very grounding or help you see things more clearly or in such a way that you don't feel stressed out by not knowing how you feel or how to approach something challenging. Journaling is also a good practice if you have vivid dreams or find yourself waking up from a dream wondering, "What the heck was that about?" It can help you unpack and explore the symbolism in a way that slows the wheels enough for you to go back to sleep. To avoid disruption from blue light on your phone, tablet, or computer, use an actual notebook.

Read. Personally, I used to read magazines to unwind, but once I started working in media and contributing to various outlets, I found that reading magazines activated my "work brain" way too much. Same goes for anything related to food, health, or cooking. My rule for reading at nighttime is "Beach Reads Only." I've found fiction or light nonfiction to be good escapes, and occasionally biographies and autobiographies, but pick whatever content is relaxing for you. Again, to avoid blue light disruption, stick with a physical book or an e-reader that does not emit blue light. If possible, keep the lights dim where you are reading as well.

Deep breathing. There are so many types of breathing exercises to try. You can simply breathe in and out slowly, or if you prefer, follow a pattern like the 4-7-8 breathing technique to help the mind and body focus on the breath rather than on what may be on your mind. To do this, close your lips and inhale for four counts. Hold your breath for seven counts. Then exhale completely through your mouth for a count of eight, making a "whoosh" sound. I'm also a fan of counting backwards from one hundred, taking a deep breath for each number.

Get out of bed. Give yourself fifteen to twenty minutes to try to go back to sleep, but if sleep continues to elude you, get out of bed and move to another area rather than drive yourself crazy tossing and turning.

Do something soothing and distracting. Once you get out of bed, do an activity that will get your mind off of your sleeplessness. Obviously, you want to be safe so this is not the time to work on a home improvement project or operate machinery, but maybe something like cleaning, organizing a drawer, or stretching.

Take a shower. A warm bath or shower can help you drift off again by lowering your core body temperature, which signals to your body that it's time to sleep. You don't need to worry about washing your hair or doing much more than rinsing off, but it can be a nice reset. As always, just be safe and make sure you've got a bathmat down to avoid slipping. Also, be careful not to fall asleep in the tub if you're bathing.

Keep your room dark and quiet. As mentioned earlier, we're very sensitive to light and sound—even when we sleep. If you find that you need your space to be darker and quieter, try blackout shades, a sleep mask, weighted eye pillows (which can be especially soothing if you hold tension in your face) and earplugs or noise cancelling headphones.

Turn to your spiritual practice. If you have a spiritual practice in your life, it can be a great source of comfort and help you feel grounded and connected. That might look like prayer, reflecting on a passage, story, or idea that calms you, or having a conversation with whomever you feel connected to on that spiritual level.

Have a snack. If you wake up and are legitimately hungry to the point where it's preventing you from falling back asleep, have a light snack to settle your stomach. Make sure it's small, low in sugar, and easy to digest. Certain foods also have compounds in them that promote restful sleep. A few patient favorites are hard boiled eggs, a spoonful of nut or seed butter, crispy chickpeas, hummus or peanut butter on toast, a banana, a piece of cheese, and golden milk (any kind of milk with turmeric, ginger, black pepper, cinnamon, and honey).

Avoid caffeine and alcohol. Caffeine and booze are two big sleep saboteurs. If you reach for a soothing cup of tea, make sure it's caffeine-free and if you need a midnight snack, go slow with chocolate if you're sensitive. Paying attention to how caffeine intake during the day impacts your sleep can also help you figure out how much is too much and when to cut yourself off. As far as alcohol is concerned, I would not recommend that as a sleep aid, as it will actually mess up your sleep cycle. It can also make you feel crummy the next morning.

CHAPTER 26

WHAT TO EAT
AND DRINK WHEN
YOU'RE EXHAUSTED

Suggested Listening: "A Whiter Shade of Pale"
—PROCOL HARUM

When you're wiped out from a lack of sleep, stress, over-whelm, or a combination, it's important to nourish your-self. While I know it can be easy to reach for coffee and carbs, being intentional about the fuel you choose can help you feel more resilient (or at least somewhat together) even when you're exhausted.

Be Prepared for Cravings

When we're short on sleep, our so-called "hunger hormones," leptin and ghrelin, go all out of whack. Because leptin impacts our perception of fullness, when we're tired, leptin levels are reduced, which means we may feel less in touch than when we're full and therefore, more likely to overeat. Ghrelin, on the other hands, regulates our perception of hunger. Sleep deprivation leads to elevated ghrelin, which can lead to feeling extra hungry or more fixated on tempting foods. Another factor often at work is that when we don't have adequate rest, our body wants help making energy and recognizes calorie-dense foods like high-fat, high-sugar foods as easy fuel, and simple carbs may be especially attractive for how quickly they digest so that glucose can enter the bloodstream. Additionally, the stress hormone cortisol, which rises when we're sleep deprived, can stimulate appetite.

Have Balanced Meals and Snacks Spread Evenly Through the Day

Having small, frequent meals and snacks is a good strategy for those tired days. Eat every three to four hours to help support stable energy and have a combination of protein, fat, and complex carbohydrates to keep you going. Carbs provide energy, and protein and fat support blood sugar management and satiety, both of which can go a long way in managing that "must eat everything in sight" compulsion that can take hold when you're exhausted. This also helps guard against energy crashes related to spikes and dips in our blood sugar and insulin levels. This is not the day to start a low-carb diet.

Some healthy meal ideas:

- a slice of whole grain toast with avocado and an egg or hemp hearts;
- a vegetable omelet and whole grain toast;
- a big salad with beans, roasted veggies, olive oil, and lemon juice; or
- a piece of baked chicken or fish with a side of cooked green veggies and roasted sweet potato.

Healthy snack ideas:

- sliced veggies with hummus or guacamole;
- plain yogurt with berries;
- piece of fruit and nuts or nut butter; or
- one hard-boiled egg and a piece of fruit.

Limit Sweets and Processed Snacks

Sugary foods and drinks as well as processed items like chips and fries can actually make you feel worse, as they provide quick calorie, carb, and fat hits but don't offer much nutritional value to help improve your energy or stabilize your mood. Stick to balanced meals and snacks to help you stay on as even a keel as possible.

Go Easy on Caffeine

You don't have to nix caffeine completely but know that over-doing it can backfire in a number of ways. For starters, it can make you jittery, and it can also mess with your sleep if you have too much or too late in the day for it to be out of your system by bedtime. It can also further dehydrate you (when you're already dehydrated from not having slept enough). If you need it, have a small cup of coffee in the morning and see if you need another mid-morning, but consider switching to black or green tea or matcha. Regardless of the form you choose, cut yourself off after 2:00 or 3:00 pm to avoid becoming too wired to settle down when it's time to go to sleep.

Hydrate, Hydrate, Hydrate

Tired cells are thirsty cells, so when you haven't slept enough, you tend to be dehydrated. This can make you feel even more tired and foggy. Have a glass of water as soon as you wake up and then a glass with and between each meal. Or if it's more helpful to think of it this way, add an extra glass or two to your usual intake.

INTERVIEW WITH DAVID "DJ" LEE

Suggested Listening: "Hands Together"
—SCRATCH TRACK

I met David "DJ" Lee, beat boxer, songwriter, performer, and producer back in 2004 or 2005 when he was part of Scratch Track, an acoustic hip-hop soul band. My dad had started managing them, and the guys used to stay at our house whenever they were in New York for shows, recordings, and meetings. Because they weren't much older than my sister and I, they kind of became our big brothers. At one time, they were on the road more days of the year than not, and DJ and his bandmates would tell us about some of the challenges of traveling so much for work. Here, he answers my questions about what he's learned from his experiences.

What are some of the physical health challenges of touring?
In my experience, it's the inconsistency, lack of routine. If we had been touring at a higher level in a bus or private jet, there may have been more, but for an indie band in a car or van, the days didn't look the same. The physical struggle was the unknown of it all. Sometimes you play at seven or you go on at midnight.

Sometimes you're traveling all day. Or sometimes timing when you can eat around travel and gigs is hard. Not to mention the food situation in terms of what's available. Does the venue provide food? Should you eat it? Are there vegetables involved? You also might not make time for exercise or movement. You might not have gotten a lot of sleep. It takes a toll.

When you're young, you feel invincible and like you can do anything. Now that I'm older, I know I have health issues with my sleep. A lot of the time we'd do overnight drives or early morning drives or right after the show drives, always being on. I have a rule now in my life where I try not to do overnight anything. It wasn't safe or wise. We tried to drink a lot of water and stay hydrated and take vitamins to keep our immune system teetering into decency. As a singer and vocalist it's important for my voice to work.

What are some of the mental and emotional challenges?

Mentally, the road will wear on you. You start to lose touch with the normalcy of community and friendship. And if you're trapped in a van with one, two, or three other people, that can wear on your psyche. I had an advantage because I'd traveled a lot as a child so I was used to being in close quarters, but there were times we wouldn't speak for three or four hours because we had nothing to say. There's a lot of downtime, a lot of waiting. Before all the social media that is so prevalent today, there was a lot more isolation.

The guys I toured with most of my career, we were pretty rooted, spiritually, and had a good foundation with family and close friends we stayed in contact with. We read books and listened to music and spent time with quality people and that helped us avoid some of the pitfalls many others deal with.

I'm aware that people energize me and give me balance and purpose. Having spiritual background and prayer helped us stay grounded. Having a root in something that is bigger than your-self matters. That extra belief and hope can help us get through every day. It can help you get out of bed and pursue happiness and goodness and love.

Is there anything you learned along the way that you have found helpful?

I wish, for the twelve years that I was in Scratch Track, that I had found time to consistently exercise, to get up earlier and make exercise part of my day. As I'm older trying to gain that flexibility and youthfulness, I know I wasn't smart. I wish I had valued the importance of exercise.

What advice would you give your younger self about health and wellness while touring? Or is there anything you wish you had known when you were just starting out?

I would encourage anyone who's going to start touring to have realistic expectations and set realistic goals and boundaries. I definitely feel like if you're about to start traveling and touring and having that lifestyle, envision what you're going to get into and have goals and boundaries around what you will or won't do. You need to know when to say no.

What is something that would surprise most people or that people get wrong about life on the road?

It's not a party. You're not on vacation. It's definitely work. Some-times you get a day off to do touristy things, but sometimes you just want to sleep.

ENERGY AND TIME MANAGEMENT

CHAPTER 27

WORKING THROUGH GUILT

Suggested Listening: "These Days" (Live)
—JACKSON BROWNE

G uilt is such an uncomfortable emotion. As my mother has always reminded me, it's a very low-vibrating one that can drag us down like no other—except maybe shame. Do you ever feel guilty when there is, in fact, nothing to truly feel guilty for? If so, I can relate to that! It's a running joke with my family and friends that I say "sorry" so much it's like punctuation.

I bring this up because, along with caregiver burnout, feelings of guilt are incredibly common in caregivers. That could look like feeling guilty for being well when they're sick or guilty for not being able to completely fix their problem, or for not being the "perfect" caregiver. Another big one is feeling guilty for spending any time or energy taking care of yourself. These are just a few examples. It's pretty incredible, the wide range of things you will wrongly find yourself feeling guilty about when you would really benefit from reminders that taking care of yourself will actually help you take better care of others.

Here are a Few Steps to Help You Start to Release Guilt Around Taking Care of Yourself

- Remind yourself in whatever way will resonate most that self-care isn't selfish.
- Reframe negative self-talk, or at least acknowledge that you're doing it and make a conscious decision not to engage with those thoughts.
- Point out to yourself all the ways in which you are doing a good job. Remind yourself that you are doing the best that you can and that that is enough.
- Get a reality check. Talk with a trusted friend, family member, or a therapist about the guilt you're feeling. Sometimes hearing yourself say it out loud or having someone reflect what you're saying back to you and put it in perspective can make you realize how that guilt is not serving you.
- Avoid spending time with negative people or people who make you feel like crap about yourself. I know this may not always be completely within your control. If there is someone you can't escape interacting with, take steps before, during, and after those interactions to calm your mind. Take a few deep breaths or repeat a mantra to yourself that helps you feel more positive.

CHAPTER 28

PROTECTING YOUR TIME AND ENERGY

Suggested Listening: "Mona Lisas and Mad Hatters"
— ELTON JOHN

S etting boundaries with your energy is vitally important, and not surprisingly, it's often incredibly difficult. In a culture where we're applauded for pushing through challenges and being productive, it's not surprising that so many of us feel pressured to keep up a breakneck pace and yet somehow make the juggling act look easy. Or when someone asks us to help with something, we're conditioned to say "Yes" even when we have limited bandwidth.

When you add a constant stream of information coming at us via our phones and computers, feelings like FOMO (fear of missing out) or of inadequacy ("why doesn't my home / dinner / body look like that?") or of obligation can creep in (like when you see that others in your network are donating time or money to a particular cause and suddenly you're whipping out your credit card or signing up to man a table even though you're not really sure what it's about).

The emotions that come up around this overload can range. Maybe you're worried about letting people down, or you're scared that if you take on less, you'll be perceived as weak, or as selfish.

Maybe you're worried that people will think you're losing your edge or, if you struggle with overcommitting to work obligations, you're scared of how it will impact your business. Logically, you probably even know that when we're spread too thin, it's much harder to do well at anything, but the idea of setting boundaries or saying "No" sounds terrifying. Or impossible.

Know that it very well may feel awkward or difficult at first. And yes, it will get better. While most of the anticipated pushback is in your head, I understand that yes, there may be some actual pushback, which is why you need to remind yourself that protecting your boundaries is not only important for your well-being but also for those who depend on you.

Here Are a Few Tips for Protecting Your Time and Energy

- Be realistic with yourself about what you actually have time and space for—and about how those things impact you. Don't forget to build in some recharge time. I am speaking from both personal and professional experience on that last part. Sure, you may have a certain number of hours in your day in which you could technically make time for something, but what does it take for you to shift gears or process? Are you cutting into your sleep or other vital self-care time?

- Decide what is and is not a priority. Especially when you are caring for someone else and have to be mindful of how your health impact your ability to care for them, this is a big one. You really can't afford to burn yourself out with stuff that doesn't serve you. Be really honest with yourself and pay attention to your gut reaction when those asks come up. Of course, there will always be those things that aren't up to you, but when it comes to what is, give this measurement tool a try: If it's not a "Hell Yes," it's a no.

- Be clear with others about what you will and won't do. When you have clear rules in place, this makes it easier. Rather than taking each situation case by case, you can fall back on, "No I can't do weekend mornings" or "I'm not taking on this kind of assignment right now, but thank you for thinking of me."
- Just say "No." Practice. Not "No, but" but actually decline. If you feel like a jerk, you can explain that you wished you could do *xyz* but can't or point the asker in the direction of someone who may be available or toward information or resources that will be useful to them. If it makes you feel better, ask them to get back in touch in the future or thank them for taking the time to ask you.
- Use a calendar to keep track of your time. Make sure to note appointments, medications, or treatments if needed, as well as things like travel time between. Don't forget about putting your self-care on there as well (sleep, workouts, cooking, etc.).
- Get organized. Establish a system for things like medications, paying bills, sorting mail, and other tasks so you can limit stress, overwhelm, and scrambling.
- Figure out what to outsource. If you're used to doing everything yourself, pay extra attention to this one. Examine why—is it coming from internal or external pressures to carry the whole load? What are you afraid will happen if you do take something off

your plate? What can you let go of? If you're having trouble coming up with something, think about your least favorite tasks or the things that feel especially torturous or time-consuming. Is there a way to delegate or at least simplify?

- Have a ritual to help you protect and cleanse your energy before and after draining situations or interactions. Whether you simply take a few deep breaths or do something like burn incense or meditate, having a simple ritual to turn to can help signal to your brain and body that you are protected and clear of any energetic "residue" you pick up through the day, and being in that mindset can make it feel a little easier to stay clear on what your boundaries are and honor them.

- Have a mood-boosting toolkit. Note what brings you joy and lifts you up when you're down. Think: music, movement, activities, laughter . . . The only "rule" is that it has to resonate with you. Knowing what you can turn to when you're in a dark place can make a huge difference in those moments where uncomfortable emotions start to throw you off course.

How to Ask for Help

Asking for help when we need it is good self-care—and even a sign of strength! I know everyone always says that and it's easy to roll your eyes about it, but it's a cliché for a reason.

Some of the most common reasons we may struggle with asking for help are that we fear being turned down or we're scared that people will think less of us for needing help. Or we just aren't used to it and feel super awkward about it. As with boundary setting, the more you do it, the easier it can get, but if you're really struggling, here are a few tips to try:

Don't apologize. Sure, asking for help may feel weird if you're not used to it, but saying "I'm sorry" won't make it any easier for either party. Think about it—apologizing upfront can make it seem like you're doing something wrong by asking for help, which is a weird energy to introduce into the conversation. Skipping the "I'm sorry, but" part can also help dial down the shame you may feel about asking.

Be specific. Think of it as making it as easy as possible for the person you're asking to help you. Let them know exactly what you need and use clear, concise language. That said, refrain from overexplaining or falling all over yourself trying to prove that you need help because you're scared someone's going to shame you for not being able to do that thing yourself.

Say "thank you." After receiving help, express your feelings of gratitude for the assistance. It will help both of you feel great. While simply saying the words is powerful, you can express your appreciation with a gift or by doing something nice for the person.

CHAPTER 29

GET ORGANIZED

Suggested Listening: "What Light"
—WILCO

One of the things I feel doesn't get talked about enough when it comes to caring for someone undergoing medical treatments or who is living with a chronic condition that requires careful management is organization. While it may never feel "easy," it can be so much easier when you get organized—this can apply both to the patient's care but also to the management of home life as well.

A lot of this extends into your own life as a caregiver, as well. For example, your ability to provide good quality care will suffer greatly if you're behind on your own household bills or your sleep, eating, and exercise are all over the place.

Coming up with systems to help keep you organized can simplify and help organization begin to feel more automatic. One of my favorites is to keep a binder where you can store documents and other materials like business cards you may need for the person you are caring for. Using dividers can help you designate areas for things such as bills, admin paperwork, educational handouts, medication fact sheets, and business cards.

Here are some tips to help you get organized. If needed, you can start with organizing one aspect at a time to make the process seem less daunting.

With Schedules

- If you've never kept a calendar before, this is a good time to start. While electronic may be easier to share with others who may be involved in the care process, if paper will be more approachable for you and help you feel more consistent, that's fine.
- Write down appointments as soon as they are scheduled. Be sure to document changes ASAP.
- If there are multiple people involved in caring for the patient, keep track of who is caring for them when. Make sure you have everybody's contact information as well. A group text thread can also be helpful for coordinating care.
- If you need to give medication daily, put that on the calendar. You may also wish to keep a hard copy of a medication schedule where you store medications.
- Don't forget to schedule your own self-care somewhere in there! Also, as you book doctor's appointments, routine screenings, and the like for yourself, make sure to put those on the calendar as well so if you need someone to cover for you, you can arrange that ahead of time. For cases where you need to go to the doctor because something acute comes up, have an arrangement in place with someone who can be available to step in.

With Treatment

- Keep an updated list of medications and supplements in an easily accessible place (such as a document that's available electronically or which you can easily print from when needed).
- Come to appointments with a list of questions for the healthcare practitioner.
- Carry a designated notebook where you can jot down questions as they come up or things you want to remember or be able to refer to later.
- Scan documents ASAP after receiving them and store them electronically in at least one other place, such as a flash drive or laptop. If it's easier, you can do this weekly, but keep in mind that waiting longer to do so could cause your memory to become hazier and increase the risk of misplacing important documents.
- Keep medications together. Keep a list with the timing and dosages of each medications. If it helps save time and energy gathering what they need, you can use a pill box.
- Keep track of dates medications were started and dates refills will be needed so you can plan ahead.

With Money

- For medical bills, keep everything in one place, such as a folder or file, where you can easily find what you need. You may wish to keep a spreadsheet of bills and note date received and the date and amount paid, as well as any other relevant information you may wish to track.

- Set reminders in your phone, if needed, to remind you to pay credit card bills, schedule payments, or withdraw money to help with daily expenses.
- If it helps lighten your mental load, set up auto payments, when you can, but designate a day each month or quarterly to review and make sure that you and the person you're caring for aren't paying for things that aren't being used.

With Household Tasks

- Don't underestimate the power of tiny daily habits to help keep an area clean. A few minutes of tidying each day (think: putting clothes in the hamper, shredding junk mail, wiping down countertops) can go a long way in preventing an overwhelming mess from accumulating.
- Have a place for everything. When you know where everything belongs, it makes the task of putting it away practically automatic.
- Set a regular cleaning schedule. Whether you do all cleaning on the same day or batch similar tasks, knowing which days you do which household tasks can help you get into the mindset to do it at the assigned time or plan around it.
- Sort mail and unpack and break down boxes from deliveries as they come in.
- Clear clutter periodically. When daily tidying isn't enough, set aside a day each week or month to de-clutter and put items in their places.
- Sign up for autoshipments and subscriptions for household goods that need to be regularly replenished.

- Outsource what you can. A good clue as to what you should seek help for are those things which you find most difficult to get done or that you just hate or don't feel up to.

With Food

- Flexible meal planning can help you figure out what you need to buy and keep on hand.
- If you're sharing cooking duties with others, keep a calendar of who's responsible for preparing food on which days.
- Set aside time for meal prep and cooking on your calendar but be realistic. Don't pressure yourself to cook a week's worth of food in one hour. On the reverse side, if it's easier to spend two or three hours on a Sunday or other day you may usually be less busy, then give yourself permission to keep things super simple during the week and just reheat things you made before.
- Embrace shortcuts like precut produce, prepared proteins, healthier frozen options, or a meal kit or healthy meal delivery service.
- Order groceries online. You can also check out subscription-based services that can save you time and energy you'd otherwise spend getting to and from a store and the time it takes to shop for and prepare food.
- Keep a list of your favorite restaurant and take-out options with healthy items you enjoy that make you feel good when you eat them.

It's Okay to Ask for Help

If you feel totally overwhelmed or need help with potentially complicated aspects of caregiving like interacting with insurance companies, you can hire a care manager. While a hospital where your loved one is receiving is a great starting place for connecting with a care manager, you can hire someone who works independently. Organizations specific to the condition your loved one has can be another good resource.

It's also okay to get outside help for things like cleaning, laundry, shopping, and errands. If budget is a factor, have a conversation with friends and family members you feel comfortable discussing it with about how to split up some of the work.

CHAPTER 30

IT'S OKAY TO LAUGH

Suggested Listening: "Starman"
—DAVID BOWIE

"Still Not Dead"
—WILLIE NELSON

As I spoke to my dad's friends and colleagues while writing this book, they all talked about his lack of interest in drugs and alcohol, despite working in a field where they were an accepted part of the culture. He'd been transparent with me growing up that, yes, he'd checked to see what the fuss was about but that it just wasn't his thing. In all honesty, this meant he had to work harder to do his job since he couldn't use cocaine as an incentive to get his artists' records played, but it wasn't something he wanted to mess around with.

I remember the drug talk as a young teen. My mom gave me the standard spiel about gateway substances, but what stuck with me were the stories my dad shared about artists he'd worked with who'd damaged their careers and lost their lives to drugs.

The idea of a substance snuffing out my inner pilot light scared the crap out of me. As so many of my classmates turned to various drugs and alcohol to numb out, I just shrugged and went back to my journal and my tarot cards. Also, I *loved* driving, and no way was I going to sacrifice that little slice of freedom. It was probably also a control thing. In college, I took a *very* short detour to learn my limits with alcohol when I turned twenty-one but got tired of that scene quickly. Since I went to a communications-focused college the first time around, I spent a lot of time around people trying to drink or blow their way to being a "real" writer or musician, and I did not want to get sucked in. So instead, I'd just stay up all night with friends watching their lines disappear and listening to their speech speed up. It was a recipe for insomnia, but that's a story for another day.

I didn't have as strong an aversion to cannabis, but it never became a regular part of my life. I only started paying attention to it as a therapeutic tool when I was working in the ALS clinic and saw how it helped with my patients' pain and other symptoms. CBD was also starting to arrive on the scene, and I was curious to study more about its uses in a medical setting.

Still, we were all a little surprised when my dad decided to try medical marijuana.

When he first started using it, it was to help with his appetite, which disappeared with the chemo. He started with rolled joints, but his fingers would cramp up so much, he couldn't light or even hold one himself. My mom had to help him. I have a memory of her one night a few weeks into his treatment, saying, "I never thought I'd say this, but I have to go help your father light a joint."

He tried a few other forms under the guidance of the dispensary staff. He liked edibles but sometimes found them too strong. The vape pen ended up working well for him. He rarely seemed "high," but could be a little extra upbeat, cracking jokes and having lively conversations. Sometimes he'd ask you random (often inappropriate) questions seemingly out of nowhere. He also seemed to have more energy, probably because his blood sugar was more stable since he could actually eat.

Because his appetite was so finicky in general as a result of the medication, he would stick to very specific foods until he needed to move on from them or had found something else that would work for a while. We put so much energy into making sure he had whatever that thing was at the ready but had to be careful not to overdo it and cause him to get overwhelmed.

Sugar continued to play a central role in my dad's diet. As I said earlier, I'd learned quickly that in order to keep the peace and have a good experience on the Farewell Tour, I needed to let go of the desire to clean up his eating. The man had been told he had terminal cancer—in the grand scheme of things, more harm than good would have come from me trying to force kale salads.

There was a phase where the main thing he ate was chocolate-covered Häagen-Dazs bars (but only the ones with chocolate ice cream inside). He also went through a mini donut phase. He especially like them warmed up. One morning I walked into the kitchen, and he had placed a tiny little donut into the microwave (without a plate underneath) and was watching it spin around. All of a sudden, there was a POP! The donut had exploded. I didn't know what to do first—laugh or freak out about him not using a plate and potentially exposing himself to germs.

He'd never been one for cooking, unless you count his signature "Greek Macaroni," which was basically ground beef and onions cooked with a can of tomatoes, seasoned with oregano, and then tossed with elbow macaroni—one of his bachelor-on-a-budget meals he'd make when my mom was working late or he needed comfort food. When the marijuana was working, though, he'd occasionally get creative in the kitchen.

One day, I was home alone with him and he wanted to make hash browns.

Neither of us had ever actually made them before, so I had to look up a recipe on my phone. When I raised my eyes, he had pulled out a cutting board and the biggest knife in the kitchen.

What coursed through me then was a glimmer of what I imagined parents felt when their toddler grips something sharp and shiny. My heart was in my mouth the whole time we prepped the potatoes and I watched him cook them over the griddle, trying not to hover over him. He wanted to do it himself, and I had to be respectful. He was the parent, after all, and I didn't want to upset him by making him feel infantilized.

I don't even remember if he ate the hash browns (sometimes his cravings passed so quickly he'd lose interest), I was just so grateful we'd gotten through the process without any cuts or burns. What I do remember is that, afterwards, we went upstairs and he watched TV while I banged out another article on the iPad mini I always had on me. The usual routine was that we'd stay that way until my mother or sister came home from work and I'd either start making dinner or catch a bus back to New York.

Why Laughter Matters

Why am I talking about all this? Something I know I struggled a lot with was whether or not it was okay to laugh, to zoom out a little and appreciate the absurdity and the humor in what would otherwise be an overwhelmingly dark time. Gallows humor has been my MO since I can remember, but during the experience of supporting my dad through cancer, I began to see that it is essential.

Laughter has physical benefits. It helps us better take in oxygen-rich air, which stimulates our organs, improves our stress response, and eases tension. It's also been shown to benefit our immune system, improve mood, and foster a sense of connection with those we laugh with.[36]

You need to make space for joy. The more accustomed we get to acknowledging what makes us happy or ignites a spark of inspiration or hope in us, the more we may be able to see it shining through the fog of our overwhelm on the difficult days.

All that said, sometimes it may not feel like you have a lot (or anything) to laugh about, so it can be helpful to be intentional about making humor a part of your life. Read funny books or ask friends for recommendations for their favorite comedy podcasts, movies, and recordings. Bookmark funny videos on YouTube or subscribe to newsletters of people whose humor resonates with you. Keep a folder on your phone or computer desktop of pictures that make you laugh. You can also ask friends to share things that make you laugh. Got people in your orbit who bum you out? This is the time to go on an unfriend / unfollow spree.

However, it's also important to respect boundaries on what's not funny to those around you. If you're not sure if it's okay to crack jokes, let the person you're caring for set the tone or ask them if you're not sure. If they're not okay with it, find a safe outlet for yourself, whether that's through appreciating humor in other areas of your life, making amusing observations in a journal, or connecting with a friend you can share some dark humor with. Another thing to consider is finding humor in things not at all related to what your loved one is going through that you can laugh at together. My family watched a lot of comedy specials on Netflix and revisited favorite funny movies together. One thing I would advise against, however, is making jokes at others' expense—in the moment it may feel good, but over time it can foster negative energy and take the joy out of that laughter.

CHAPTER 31

HOW TO SHIFT
YOUR ENERGY

Suggested Listening: "Small Town Moon"
—REGINA SPECTOR

Have you ever noticed that when you get into a down mood or an angry mood, it can color every interaction you have and drag down your whole day? Our energy is powerful. Sometimes it feels aligned with the situation we find ourselves in, but sometimes we find that we need to shift and get into a more positive energy flow to feel back on track. Here are a few of my favorite tools to help you make that change. Pick one or two to try—or try as many as you like.

Use movement. Exercise is one of the best tools we have available to shift our energy—and it doesn't have to cost a damn thing. It doesn't have to be formal exercise either. Even a short walk or a stretch can help us feel better.

Use your words. The words we say, write, and even read hold tremendous power. Pay attention to the words you use to describe a situation. Chances are that if you're using lots of negative words or describing what's going on with you in very negative terms, you're going to feel more negative. Practice catching yourself in the moment and reframing those thoughts and replacing those words with ones that land a little more softly. You could also try writing positive affirmations in a journal or writing (and even sending) yourself a note of encouragement. Another of my favorite tips? Choose a word that aligns with how you want to feel and incorporate it into your passwords or make a graphic or write it on a Post-it and put it in a place you'll see through the day.

Use a mantra. Choosing a mantra to repeat when you start to feel overwhelmed is a great way to refocus your energy. You can take inspiration from quotes that speak to you or come up with something all your own. Nobody has to know about it, but if it feels empowering to share it with someone, you certainly can share that this is something you're working with.

Use music. Music is another of my favorite ways to change your energy frequency. Notice which songs make you feel different ways. If you like, you can make playlists with different themes that you can listen to when needed.

Use color. It's a subtle but powerful tool. Colors can have very distinct effects on our mood, and when we tune into that, we can become familiar with how we can use exposure to different colors to lift us up, calm us down, or energize us. This isn't anything new—color therapy (aka chromotherapy) is believed to have been practiced in Ancient Egypt and Greece. While there isn't a ton of clinical data on the psychological and biological effects of color on humans, you've likely noticed that you respond differently to various colors and associate them with certain emotions and sensations. One way to utilize color therapy in everyday life is to wear colors that reflect how you want to feel or choose accessories in that color. You can also play around with changing light bulbs or changing up your nail color or even hair color for a fun change of pace.

Use light, which also plays a role in how we feel. Have you ever noticed changes in your mood or energy as the weather and light change? Though research is ongoing, light therapy has been studied for its potential to help boost mood and even treat seasonal affective disorder. Just be mindful that exposure to bright light (and blue light from electronics, especially) too close to bedtime can disrupt sleep.

Use scent. Smell can trigger so much emotion and so many memories. While it can be very personal, research has shown that certain scents seem to have specific effects. Lavender, for example, has been shown to be calming, peppermint to be helpful for focusing and energizing, and citrus to be uplifting, just to name a few. If there is a scent you feel especially drawn to, consider purchasing an essential oil you can keep handy so you can reach for it when needed.

Use your breath. Breath work is another free thing you can use shift your energy. Research has shown that even a small amount can have a meaningful impact.

Use meditation. It costs absolutely nothing and yet has been shown to offer tremendous benefit to the mind and body. Rather than pressure yourself to completely empty your mind, focus on quieting the chatter or clearing some space. There are many forms of meditation, so find one that speaks to you to start with. For example, you could try a guided meditation or set a timer for the period of time you want to meditate and either close your eyes or pick something to focus on, like a candle or a spot on the floor in front of you.

Use a journal. A journal can make a great safe space in which to vent or to explore your feelings or even soothe yourself. You definitely don't have to share it with anybody or even tell anyone that you keep a journal, but it's another great tool to have.

Use laughter. It really is good medicine. It can help relieve tension, release feel-good endorphins, and foster a sense of connection with others.

CHAPTER 32

CULTIVATING MINDFULNESS WHEN YOU HAVE MINIMAL TIME

Suggested Listening: "I'll Be Here in the Morning"
—TOWNES VAN ZANDT

M indfulness is another valuable tool we have available to help us navigate challenging times. Maybe you've even had a healthcare practitioner, family member, or friend recommend it to you.

So what exactly is mindfulness? In this context, mindfulness is (according to the Oxford English Dictionary) "a mental state achieved by focusing one's awareness on the present moment, while calmly acknowledging and accepting one's feelings, thoughts, and bodily sensations, used as a therapeutic technique."

There are even therapeutic techniques specifically centered around mindfulness, such as Mindfulness-Based Stress Reduction (MBSR), which was created by Dr. Jon Kabat-Zinn in the 1970s. It incorporates yoga and meditation to help people address the unconscious behaviors, feelings, and thoughts contributing to their stress and related health issues. Mindfulness-Based Cognitive Therapy (MBCT) is a type of psychotherapy that combines cognitive behavioral techniques with mindfulness strategies like meditation, yoga, and mindfulness practices that help you become more aware in the present moment.

There are so many ways to practice mindfulness in your everyday life, even when you feel like you have no time and get irritated by the suggestion that you "try to relax," "limit stress," or "take a deep breath."

That said, a deep breath can be incredibly grounding, and those times you feel like you can't possibly pause to take in that extra oxygen is probably when you need it most.

Here are a few simple ways to cultivate mindfulness:

Try breath work. Whether it's a simple deep breath a few times a day, or a specific breath work exercise like box breathing, alternative nostril breathing, or another exercise that speaks to you. Box breathing, also called "square breathing," is a technique used to boost concentration, focus, and performance by taking very slow, deep breaths. First, you slowly exhale completely, and then inhale through your nose for a very slow count to four, feeling the air fill your lungs, section by section, and into your abdomen. Then you hold your breath for four seconds before exhaling slowly again, focusing on the air leaving your lungs and abdomen. Finally, hold your breath for a count of four again and repeat the cycle. Alternate nostril breathing is a yogic breath control practice that involves plugging each nostril in a pattern as you inhale and exhale through your nose. There are lots of helpful online tutorials to guide you through this practice.

Meditate. Even one minute of meditation can help. Use whichever technique helps you best get into that calmer mental state. Start with an app if you like having guidance. Having trouble incorporating it into your routine? Attach it to something you already do every day.

Pause before eating. Taking a moment to look at and smell your food is a great way to tune in and eat more mindfully, which is great for the mind and body.

Walk without listening to music, podcasts, or talking on the phone. Limiting distractions and letting yourself take in the scenery around you will help you feel more connected to your surroundings.

Practice yoga or another form of mindful movement for a few minutes per day or a few times per week.

Journal. If it feels good, just write freely about whatever is on your mind, but if you find it more useful, you can use journal prompts.

Sit quietly without distractions. Being surrounded by lots of noise, images, or activity can make it hard to quiet the mind and become aware. Even if it is in those few moments before bed, take a few moments to be in the quiet.

INTERVIEW WITH
BILLY KEANE

Suggested Listening: "*Wild Wide Open Spaces (Live)*"
—WHISKEY TREATY ROADSHOW

I first met singer-songwriter Billy Keane in 2013 when my dad was working with him in New York, introducing him to producers and setting him up with industry people and having him write with Willie Nile, whom you'll hear from later in the book. Billy and my dad had been introduced through James Taylor, another artist with whom my dad worked closely during his time at Columbia and after.

While I lost track of Billy after he and my dad stopped working together, we randomly reconnected in 2019, almost a year after my dad's death, when my then-boyfriend, now-husband invited me on a road trip to Massachusetts for a work event. The company he worked for was sponsoring this band, The Whiskey Treaty Roadshow, and Jacob had to go up and batch cocktails to serve during a show. He'd made friends with the band and thought I would love their music.

On the drive up, a text message popped up on the navigator from someone named Billy Keane. Why did I know that name? It bothered me for hours until it finally dawned on me. What were the chances, though?

"Ask him if he knows the name Rocky Del Balzo," I told Jacob.

Sure enough, it was the same Billy Keane I'd first met on the Lower East Side before a gig at the Rockwood Music Hall. It was such a strange and lovely coincidence.

When Jacob proposed the following winter in Central Park, he surprised the hell out of me by inviting Billy and his bandmate, Tory Hanna, to be there, playing their guitars by the Bethesda Fountain as he popped the question.

When I interviewed Billy about his touring experience, we agreed we couldn't not tell that story. I still get goosebumps when I think about it.

What are some of the physical health challenges of touring?

"Touring" encompasses so many experiences. Whether you're just starting out or a decade into it, the finances are always going to be a primary consideration, especially when it comes to diet! If venues are putting up meals, you're not talking about the best curated healthy food. The real-life temptations you're facing are compounding.

The biggest challenge for me was quitting drinking, but it was one of the best decisions I made in my life.

You have the musician persona and then you have to be a person, and on the tour the line gets blurred. It's a true health risk, physical and mental. There's this mythology that goes with being a musician and what that lifestyle entails.

A lot of musicians go onstage and if your persona is extroverted and you're an introverted person, sometimes drinking is the easiest way to do that. Advice for a younger Billy would be, "Sober up, focus more on your art and less on your lifestyle."

After I quit, my manager had to put in our rider that we don't drink anymore so people don't buy us shots.

A consideration when we're on the road is staying healthy. If you blow yourself out the first few nights but you still have two, three weeks that's no good. Not partying all night, every night is really important. And drink lots of water. The guys who have been touring a long time and are healthy all have routines.

It's not vacation, you're working. You have to take the same level of care as when you're home. Even more is probably necessary. Personally, I just try and maintain. I've got a pretty regimented workout schedule when I'm home and on the road I try to keep a certain routine going.

What are some of the mental and emotional challenges?

Personally, I love it. In a normal year we'll go out for a few weeks in spurts. Some musicians though are out there for 250 dates per year, which can be a little unsettling. A lot of relationships struggle.

When I'm out there, I'm focused on the music in a way that's really healthy for me. It feels like home. The guys with families it's more challenging. Sometimes the family comes. You just figure it out, but you miss being home.

What advice would you give to artists about health and wellness while touring? Or is there anything you wish you had known when you were just starting out?

Take it easy on drinking. That's advice that I think umbrellas so much other advice. A lot of musicians start touring when they're young and their body can take a whole lot. It's amazing how quickly that changes. Even holding my guitar for hours, now, I get a sore back, and my wrists and hands get sore.

There are people who are giving TED talks about ergonomic practices for musicians to make sure your body stays okay. Pay attention because it's not going to be an issue now but will be later. Plan for the future.

As a young musician I was not planning. I was just playing music and doing what I could to play more music. As you get older you realize the consequence of that "dive in head-first" mentality. There needs to be some awareness in order for there to be longevity. Nobody is a superhero. Everybody is just a person. Some people are bigger than life onstage, but nobody is bigger than life in reality. There are mythologies that get built around people and we lean into that rather than leaning into bettering ourselves.

What is something that would surprise most people or that people get wrong about life on the road?

I think people don't understand the amount of prep it takes to put on a show, even the ones that appear to be casual. The preparation is anything but casual. You're prepping, you're honing your craft, you're setting up the stage. Everybody has their role to play behind the scenes. But I do think people don't know about the level of prep that goes into it. From my experience you curate the heck out of it and focus on presenting it the audience in a way that requires a lot of attention to detail.

SPIRITUALITY

CHAPTER 33

THE NEW CATHOLIC

Suggested Listening: "American Without Tears"
—ELVIS COSTELLO

"Birds (Live at the Cellar Door"
—NEIL YOUNG

I knew my father had accepted he was dying when he converted to Catholicism.

My entire life, my dad, who was (nonpracticing) Greek Orthodox, had made it very well known that he was only doing it to make my mom happy when he joined us for mass on a holiday or for a family event like a christening or communion. If he'd ever had any problem with my mother wanting to raise my sister and I with Catholicism as our frame of reference, I never heard anything about it, but I do know he certainly wasn't enthusiastic about participating.

What I grew up being told was that my mom wanted us to have the information and to understand our family heritage, and then to make up our own minds. My dad had always said he was, "spiritual but not religious." That made sense to me. There was a lot that didn't feel good to me about the particular parish I was raised in, but I was curious about religion. When my grandmother died when I was thirteen, as I was getting ready to make my confirmation, that curiosity intensified, as did my sense of mortality. This was around the same period where I used to lie awake at night worrying about the apocalypse.

One time my dad found me in a closet with a giant book in my lap.

"What's that?"

"A Bible."

"I didn't even know we had one."

"I'm looking for the Book of Revelation."

"Why the hell do you want to do that?"

I shrugged and put the book back. It certainly wouldn't help my sleep.

I assumed his resistance to organized religion and the Catholic Church in particular, had to do with the fact that he and my mom's father had a very strained relationship. My grandfather was the kind of devout Catholic who made donations in your name to religious organizations as a birthday gift. I saw my dad's resistance to sharing his religion as a subtle act of rebellion; my grandfather was scary when I was a kid, and I liked that my dad wasn't afraid of him.

Oddly, my grandfather died only a few months before my father. He had been battling Alzheimer's dementia for several years. The earliest sign, in fact, had been that he'd started being nice to my father, causing us to joke that "Wow, something must really be wrong with him. It's like he's forgotten he hates him!" Well, it turned out there was a medical reason for that, and as my grandfather's condition advanced, it actually enabled him and my father to have a peaceful relationship, which was healing for my mother too.

I got the news about his passing at the end of March 2018, when I was in New Orleans on a work trip. The whole time I was there, I had the Elvis Costello song, "American Without Tears" stuck in my head on a loop—in part because the song mentions

NOLA, but also because I found myself unable to cry. All the stress we'd been under had left me numb.

At the funeral, my dad stayed in the car while I walked with my mom to the gravesite, the two of us huddled under a black umbrella. We didn't want to say what we were both feeling. This was practice.

When my dad first announced a few weeks later that he wanted to convert to Catholicism, I legitimately thought he was joking. It was basically the last thing I'd ever expected him to say. When I realized he was serious, I asked what had made him decide to join the club. He explained that he wanted us all to be the same religion—and to be able to have a proper funeral in the church where so many family events had taken place.

Typically, there are a lot of steps and education involved in converting to Catholicism, but given the circumstances (and his thirty-six years of marriage to a Catholic, I suppose), he was welcomed in on a spring weekday morning. One of my few regrets in life is that I listened to him when he said not to come for the short ceremony—it's a memory I'd like to have a visual for. He did tell me about it later over the phone, though.

"I walked out of the church," he laughed, "and I said, 'Now that's *two* religions I'm not practicing!'"

Even though he was cracking jokes about being The New Catholic, I wondered how he was really feeling. We didn't talk much about his faith, though he did like to tell the story of when he and my mother met with a priest in preparation for their church wedding in 1981.

He'd told me the story many times over the years: "There was a question on this worksheet they gave us that said, 'My thoughts on Jesus Christ are . . .' and then a big blank space where you were supposed to write those thoughts. I just put, 'infrequent.'"

* * *

I feel like my sister and I benefited from growing up with friends from all different faith backgrounds and being encouraged to keep an open mind and pay attention to what truly resonated with us, even as we went through the Catholic rituals of baptism, communion, and confirmation. There were plenty of times I questioned what might be out there or up there, but I have had a few experiences that really solidified for me that I did believe in something beyond what we can see.

One I'll share happened the summer I was twenty-seven. I was working my first job out of grad school and totally burned out. I was sad and lonely after a breakup that had had a lot to do with that person not being able to handle my work schedule. All my friends were pairing off and I was questioning everything. Working in subacute rehab and long-term care (I covered both a pediatric and a geriatric unit) had me thinking a lot of dark thoughts about whether I should even bother with having children but also what might happen to me if I lived the rest of my life without finding a partner or having a family. And then in the middle of it, a friend died from cancer—someone so young and talented and kind. I felt surrounded by pain and darkness and I had no idea how to find my way out. I could barely sleep for the nightmares.

I used to wander down to this basement room in the facility where they kept all the uniforms. It was quiet and warm and the overhead light was never on, so it always felt calmer. I'd just stand there and soak it in for a moment until I had to rush back to whatever nutrition emergency was lighting up my pager.

That summer I started seeing feathers everywhere. Sure, on the sidewalk, but then I started seeing them in strange places: on a seat in the subway, outside my apartment door, on an Amtrak train, in a restaurant bathroom. People who believe in signs will often say that finding things in your path like coins and feathers are a way in which someone who has passed might say hello, so in a weird way, it was comforting, but I still felt lost.

One day we got a new admit on the geriatric subacute unit. This woman had flatlined the week before and then come to our facility to recuperate. Her eyes were totally clouded over with cataracts. I'd never seen anything like it. As I began to ask her the usual intake questions, I was soothed by her warm voice.

"They tell me I died last week," she said. "I guess I just wasn't ready to go."

"Welcome back," I said.

"I'm glad to be back, I suppose. I just wish the food was better."

I told her I'd do my best to get the food service program to honor her preferences and asked her to share about what she liked to eat.

A few minutes into our conversation, she changed the subject. "Tell me, Jessica," she said, "are you a spiritual person?"

Wow. I looked down to gather my thoughts, and there at my feet was a tiny feather.

"Yes," I said.

CHAPTER 34

THE ROLE OF SPIRITUALITY IN WELLNESS

Suggested Listening: "White Winter Hymnal"
— FLEET FOXES

"Rivers and Roads"
— THE HEAD AND THE HEART

I don't know if I could do my work as a dietitian and health coach and not believe there is something beyond what we can see. As I mentioned earlier, technically, I was raised Catholic, but I have never felt connected to just one organized religion, maybe because it's never felt as much about belonging to a particular religion than it has about feeling connected to something bigger and nurturing the spirit on a deeper, more individualized level. I know some people may call that a cop-out (growing up I heard the term "cafeteria Catholic" used in a disparaging way by some judgmental friends whose mothers clearly talked smack about my "weird" family), but I've always found comfort in the statement "take what you need and leave the rest."

Spiritual wellness can be an important piece of the big picture, and it can look different for everyone. At its core, though, it has a lot to do with feeling connected with your life's meaning and purpose, and with understanding what values and beliefs your actions stem from. While numerous studies have shown that having some sort of spiritual belief is associated with improved mental and physical health, it's not about following a particular religion or worshiping at a particular venue in a particular way. It's not about being "good."

Maybe because of how I grew up, I'm less concerned about what's "right" or "correct," and more concerned with what someone draws from their faith or spiritual practice. What brings comfort and hope? What keeps you going when you feel scared or tired? What or whom do you pray to in the middle of the night or thank for a beautiful sunrise?

There are different things we seek and find in spiritual and religious practices. Almost every health expert I interviewed for this book mentioned spirituality. Regardless of whether you were brought up around religion or not, when you are in a caregiving role, it's worth exploring your own thoughts about spirituality and noticing what you feel drawn toward or away from and why.

A few tips for getting started:

- Reflect on what your experience with (or lack thereof) spirituality was like growing up. What resonated with you? What did not?
- What ideas or practices resonate with you now?
- If there is a particular religion you identify with, what do you like about it?
- What do you find comforting?
- What makes you feel connected to others?

As for my dad's new religion, he didn't start going to church regularly, but converting did bring him and my mother some comfort, she explained. "Those are the comforting rituals you go to in hard times, and I guess he instinctively knew that."

She shared that he didn't like to talk a lot about what might be next, and he didn't have a big plan for what he wanted to wear or what poems he wanted read at his funeral or where he wanted to be buried or anything like that, but they had their own practices that allowed them to connect and find peace. "When we would drive into the city, he would make playlists and we would talk about them. Music was incredibly important to both of us. He says hello to me with music now, which I find a great comfort. It was a big part of our lives."

Fostering Connection

One of the biggest challenges of being a caregiver is isolation. This can be related to physical isolation, feeling emotionally isolated, or a combination. What is frustrating about this is that that's probably one of the times you can most benefit from connection, but even the idea of making time or of giving energy to others can feel overwhelming.

I spoke with Daisy Mack, who is the founder of Spiritual Mixtape. A self-described corporate dropout who worked in the music industry before jumping ship, she is now a breath work and stress management expert as well as an integrative nutrition health coach and yoga teacher. Connection, she explained, is vital to overall well-being. "It provides meaning. As humans, whether we choose to acknowledge it or not, we have to live in a place where our lives mean something more than the everyday."

As a caregiver, connection can be especially helpful. "Knowing that other people understand the pain you're going through is deeply part of the healing and helps you go through another day. It can be really depleting if you don't have other people saying, 'I see your story, I get it. I feel that too.' It feels good to have a shared story."

Here are a few places to start:

- Give yourself permission to take connection at whatever pace you need.
- Designate a relative or friend to reach out on your behalf.
- Consider starting an online page like Carebridge where you can share updates about what you and the person you're caring for are going through so people can follow along and respond and show their support.
- Consider a support group.
- Spend time in nature.
- Practice deep breathing or meditation to help you feel more connected to yourself.
- If you have a spiritual practice, attend a physical or virtual service or spend time in prayer or meditation.

There is no "one size fits all" with this. You really do just need to honor where you're at.

CHAPTER 35

ALL YOUR
FAVORITE BANDS

Suggested Listening: "All Your Favorite Bands"
— D A W E S

M y dad was always listening to new-to-him music. One thing we found a lot of common ground on was alt-country and folk-rock, often bands we were introduced to at the Newport Folk Festival, our version of an (almost) yearly family vacation. The first time we went was 2005, when my mother had guessed correctly that my life would be vastly enriched by seeing the Pixies (not even remotely folksy, but one of my all-time favorite bands) play an acoustic version of "Gigantic" and watching my dad squirm and cover his ears at the lyrics.

Okay, so maybe we couldn't listen to the Pixies together, but we got to share a lot of other musical experiences together. A few that stand out to me in that folk-ish category (just to name a few, in no specific order) are: Shakey Graves, Spirit Family Reunion, the Decemberists, the Milk Carton Kids, the Head and the Heart, Jason Isbell, Langhorne Slim, Alabama Shakes, the Lone Bellow, Nathaniel Rateliff & the Night Sweats, Brett Dennen, the Lumineers, Fleet Foxes, and the Avett Brothers.

Of course, we listened to a bunch of the classics: I grew up on the Beatles, Elton John, Bob Dylan, Crosby, Stills, Nash & Young, Simon and Garfunkel, and when I was a little older, the Rolling Stones, Elvis Costello, and Tom Waits. Bruce Springsteen because, well, New Jersey. I will always have a soft spot for Steve Goodman's goofier songs like "Chicken Cordon Blues" and "Vegematic." Throughout my dad's illness, we joked about arranging a Mets version of the funeral described in Goodman's "A Dying Cubs Fan's Last Request." When my husband and I first got to those early stages of listening to music together, we were both shocked that the other not only knew the song "City of New Orleans" but also that Goodman had written and recorded it before it was famously covered by Arlo Guthrie and Willie Nelson. Even though we had long aged out of counting shared musical taste as a reliable indicator of compatibility, it was something we bonded over.

My parents had a huge collection of records and CDs from my dad's work, so whenever I got curious about an artist, I would dig into the archives, going as deep as I needed to satisfy my curiosity. My brain still works in seasons and albums. Whenever I feel like a cat that's climbed to the top of a tall tree, I know that listening to Paul Simon's "American Tune" will bring me back down but that if I so much as even think about listening to any of Leonard Cohen's earlier songs, I'm going to be up there a while.

A band my dad really enjoyed listening to in the last few months of his life was Dawes. I remember hearing a lot of their songs on his Spotify playlists. That's how I was introduced to them. Watching my parents listen to music together was so freaking adorable.

A couple weeks before my dad passed away, we went to the Jersey Shore. On the way home at the end of the weekend, my parents started bickering about random stuff. I was sitting in the backseat as we made our way up the Garden State Parkway, staring out the window at the dusky highway, just trying to mentally prepare myself for a busy week ahead.

All of a sudden, Dawes' "All Your Favorite Bands" came on the stereo, and my parents stopped arguing and just sang along through the whole song. Even though it had just gotten dark, I left my sunglasses on because I didn't want them to see me cry.

RELATIONSHIPS

CHAPTER 36

ACCEPT THAT YOUR RELATIONSHIPS WILL CHANGE

Suggested Listening: "Turn! Turn! Turn! (To Everything There is a Season)"
—THE BYRDS

Something I wish someone had told me when I was first adjusting to the new normal of my dad's illness was that *your relationships will change*. This may include friendships, family relationships, professional relationships, and romantic relations. Your relationship with yourself will also change. That doesn't have to be a bad thing, but if you don't acknowledge the shift or if you try too hard to fight it, the pain may be worse. Your perspective changes. Your energy changes. Your emotions are different. You're dealing with more stress and less time.

If you've been trying to uphold certain rhythms and balances in your relationships, be aware that things could start to look very different—and that's okay. Give yourself permission to set boundaries, and when it matters, communicate clearly about what others in your life can expect from you.

For example, if you were previously doing an employee carpool but you have to duck out because you need to be able to be flexible to take the person you're caring for to appointments, check in on them during your break, or get to them ASAP at the end of your workday so you can relieve the person helping them during your workday, you need to communicate that. Yes, you may feel you're missing out on inside jokes, gossip, or bonding moments, and it's also okay to acknowledge and process those emotions.

Another example: If you typically help a friend, co-worker, or neighbor with something but you no longer have the bandwidth to do it all, if you try to keep doing it on top of all the new responsibilities you have, you run the risk of starting to feel resentful of that person. I would strongly recommend communicating clearly with them that your schedule has changed and that you will be less available.

If you're dating, what you are looking for and what you need from a partner will be different from what you needed before you were in a caregiver role. Check in with yourself along the way and give yourself some space as you adjust.

If you're in a romantic relationship, things are going to change, and communication is key. Keep each other in the loop about what you're feeling, what you're struggling with, and how you can support one another. This may include finding ways to nurture intimacy when your time and energy are limited, reevaluating the division of household responsibilities, dealing with emotional ups and downs one or both of you may be experiencing, and more. If it is helpful, consult with a counselor as you navigate the issues that come up and how they impact your relationship.

CHAPTER 37

SHOULD YOU DATE?

Suggested Listening: "All I Really Want to Do
(Live at Philharmonic, 1964)"
— BOB DYLAN

A question I had when we were supporting my dad through his cancer journey was, "Should I be dating right now?" I was so wiped on weeknights, and weekends with my family were so precious, and I certainly wasn't in the right headspace to meet my future spouse, but as the months went on, sometimes I'd panic about whether I'd later wish I had sucked it up and tried harder. I was thirty-one when my father was diagnosed, and then my *younger* sister got married. Even though I knew better, it messed with my head.

Because I am no expert on dating, I wanted to interview someone who is. Lily Womble is a dating coach and the founder of Date Brazen. I first met Lily at a Six Degrees Society event I was speaking at in New York City. I'd just started recording episodes for my then-upcoming podcast, *Drama-Free Healthy Living*, and after a brief chat in which she told me about her work, I knew I wanted to have her on as a guest. I appreciate her self-compassionate yet no-nonsense approach.

Should You Date if You're a Caregiver?

When I asked Womble about whether it's okay to date when you're in a caregiver role, she shared that there is no one right answer. "I think it depends on where you're at in that journey and what support you have as a caregiver," she says. "I've spoken to single women who don't get much support from anyone else. They are the main caregiver and their head is underwater trying to take care of their family member and themselves in a basic way. If that is where you're at, I don't recommend dating when you're submerged."

However, she adds, "if you have others to lean on and you are working to prioritize your personal life, if that is an active project in your life, then dating can be an amazing way to invest in yourself and in what you prioritize."

Dating Do's for Caregivers

If you do decide to date, says Womble, there are a few important things to consider. "Very tactically, practically, time is something you need to keep in mind." She also recommends looking at what support you need to make time in your schedule to work on your dating life.

She also encourages being super-clear on what, exactly, you hope to get out of dating during that time. "Are you looking for a life partner, a just-for-fun partner? A hookup buddy? You need to know that and let that intention spark your actions. If you're looking for a partner, open yourself up to it and think about what it would look like for you to be in that relationship and allow someone else to show up for you and with you."

Something to watch out for, she says, is having a hard time receiving help and support or feeling guilty about focusing energy on this part of your life. "Caregivers may be so used to giving support, they may struggle receiving it."

However, it's important to call out bad behavior. "What allowances are you willing to make for people?" she asks. This is where noticing your own mindset blocks and how they manifest in your life can be helpful. "Some people get into pen pal relationships on dating apps or spend so much time seeing someone they know isn't right for them. The scarcity fear behind that is indicative of a deeper issue around self-worth and whether you are allowed to want what you want. Are you willing to give yourself permission to want what you want and find the time to go after it?"

Speaking of dating apps, said Womble, "Dating apps are not the answer to your dating life." For people who are exhausted at the end of the day, she explained, "there is sometimes this misconception that dating apps should be easy."

In reality, she explained, "Intentional efforts yield intentional results. A dating app is not the answer to anyone's dating life. It's a tool to help you get to know your dating personality and to meet someone outside your social circle." You can still use dating apps, but "begin with an intentional strategy." For example, she said, you could spend twenty minutes per day at a time when you actually have energy and time to swipe and message people.

She is not a fan of the "Numbers Game" mentality around dating apps. Buying into the idea that you must go on as many dates as possible, she said, "is suggesting that your time is not very valuable and you can't trust your instincts. It also leads most people to feel burnt out." Not helpful when you're a caregiver and already prone to burnout.

If you're dating and find yourself in a situation that doesn't feel so great, says Womble, "sit down with yourself and acknowledge what doesn't feel good, where you do and don't feel supported, and what your dream scenario would be." It can also help, she adds, to have the conversation with yourself of "Why am I in this right now? What deep fear is this behavior stemming from?" She says to choose "a useful and true thought" (as opposed to just beating up on yourself and to give yourself permission to feel the way you want to feel. "Then take action."

By the way, working on your dating life doesn't have to be just about going on dates. Womble explains, "Working on your dating life can also mean going to therapy, journaling about your deepest desires, and practicing self-compassion."

Prioritize Your Relationship with Yourself

I'm sure I'm not the first person you've heard this from, but the relationship you have with yourself is the most important. All others flow from there.

This comes into even sharper focus when you're dating. "Dating is a microcosm of every hope, dream, fear, insecurity, and desire we have as human beings," says Womble. "It's important to dig beneath the surface and look at the disconnect between what you say you want and what you accept. When someone does the inner work on themselves, that directly impacts the matches they attract. It's about standing firm in who you are and what you want."

Here are a few of her tips for working on your relationship with yourself during a time where you're very focused on caring for someone else:

Show yourself some compassion. "I think the number one tool is self-compassion," says Womble. That can be "learning how to turn toward yourself as a friend would and say, 'I hear you, I see you, I'm here for you.'" She adds, it's also about learning how to let yourself be enough wherever you're at.

Be mindful. "Another tool I practice is mindfulness," says Womble. Another big one is what she calls "thought work." For example, part of this work is acknowledging that your thoughts are not facts. "If you're having thoughts about how you'll never find someone because you're too busy or don't deserve that, take a step back and acknowledge that that thought is not a fact."

Focus on thoughts that are useful and true. Building on that thought work and mindfulness, explains Womble, is focusing on thoughts that are "useful and true." If you desire a partner, she says, and are a caregiver, and you're having a self-defeating thought about your situation, "you don't have to jump immediately to the most positive thought if it doesn't feel useful or true. Take baby steps with yourself." Acknowledge the thoughts that come up, she says, "then choose one that feels useful and true. For example, acknowledging that you're on your path" and that that in and of itself is significant.

CHAPTER 38

I'LL TRY TO SWING BY

Suggested Listening: "Tell Me Why"
—NEIL YOUNG

"Goodmorning"
—BLEACHERS

My dad set the bar high with relationships. He worshipped my mother. He always said if you love someone you should tell them—and tell them every five minutes. Don't be afraid or ashamed to have feelings. It sounded great, but I couldn't seem to make that advice stick.

My dating life was a tricky subject in my family. The dark glow of the PTSD that made it hard for me to see clearly in relationships was an open well we tiptoed around. My introduction to sex and relationships had been an unhappy and violent one. As a teenager and into my twenties, I'd felt pressured to just get over it, but I've always been one to pick at scabs, so this proved challenging.

For a long time, my dad and I fought about it. I didn't want to shove all the hurt down, and at the time, I really couldn't hold space for how hard it must have been as a parent to see your child trying to process something you couldn't fix, so I just leaned into my anger. Because we were similarly stubborn, we locked horns if the topic ever came up.

I have to credit my mother with helping us heal that part of our relationship. One morning on a family vacation when I was twenty-seven, my dad and I had an argument and my mother locked us out of the house. She told us to go on a walk and to not come back until we'd talked it out—and we did. We got to a place where we had both said what we needed to and understood where the other was coming from, a certain peace and understanding from that point on that allowed us to get on well.

Still, by the time I got into my early thirties, after a few false starts, I remained afraid to relax into a healthy romantic relationship. When my dad was diagnosed, it felt like a weird vacation from my PTSD and from all the shame I'd been lugging around. Logically, I knew it would probably still be waiting for me on the other side (much as I hated to think about "the other side" being after my dad had passed), but I felt a strange freedom. In terms of dating, there was just so much less to care about now that most of my anxieties were focused on my father's health and not on whether I was too much or not enough for a romantic partner.

As I mentioned at the very beginning of this book, at the time of my dad's diagnosis, I was very single and very focused on my career, and I was forced to admit that I'd been closing myself off and numbing out with work. It was kind of a relief to admit that I missed human connection. I didn't need to meet my *person* yet. In fact, the idea of bringing someone significant into the picture during such an uncertain, stressful time seemed like a bad idea since I knew how attached my parents could get to the idea of a stable boyfriend for me. But I was tired of feeling so disconnected from desire. I needed to remember what it felt like to be alive in that way.

On the ride back to the city the morning after my parents broke the news, rather than text my girlfriends about what was going on with my dad, I reached out to a guy friend I'd known for a few years. We'd go out for drinks now and then, maybe make out on occasion, but he'd never pressured me for more. At that time, he was still into nonmonogamy. For the entire time we'd known each other, I'd made it very clear that I was only looking to get physical with someone I could be monogamous with (I learned early on that I'm old-fashioned like that—I think it's the same wiring that makes me find tapas really dissatisfying), and he respected that without question, though he'd made it equally clear that if I ever changed my mind, he'd be there.

I was sweating a little as I typed out the message. I filled him in on what was going on with my dad and asked if he was free to get drinks that night. I also told him I was ready to take him up on his offer, if it still stood. It did.

Having someone I could both talk to honestly about the tough stuff but also laugh with and let off steam with, physically, really got me through that summer. It was totally worth risking the oxytocin crushes that often break up friendships. We were always pretty sober and very safe and there was never any drama. An occasional night off the Cancer Tour helped me feel normal again, even if only for a few hours.

That said, I was relieved that fall when he decided to become exclusive with one of the women he'd been seeing—someone he'd later end up marrying. I'd had some anxiety about things ending poorly between us one day, and now we could just go back to being friends without the physical part. Throughout my dad's illness and long after, he continued to be a regular part of my friend network.

It was a few months later, though, where I made things complicated for myself with someone else. We'll call him Mark because I never actually dated anyone named Mark. We'd been in each other's orbit for a few years but had never actually gone for the drink we said we would, until one freezing Sunday when we finally did.

It was one of those things that starts between friends over whiskey and then leads to a lot of overthinking. To say that I was just looking to have fun wouldn't be quite accurate. In retrospect, it was a bit more medicinal for me than that. We could technically see other people, which was usually fine with me until it wasn't.

Every other time I saw Mark I showed up with the intention to break things off, but I just couldn't pull the trigger. The idea of trying to meet someone new and possibly getting my heart broken as I watched my dad waste away scared me into sticking with the familiar. At least with Mark I knew I could *expect* to end up feeling bad about myself. And of course, well, oxytocin is a very powerful drug. Once the buzz had worn off, I'd typically descend into a shame spiral about messing around with someone who felt so casual about me when that wasn't what I really wanted, but at least it was a predictable cycle.

Suddenly January became August, which was about to bleed into September. I was emotionally and physically exhausted from packing my suitcase every weekend to be with my family and dropping everything in the middle of the workweek to take my dad to doctor's appointments.

Mark had made it clear from the beginning, in his way, not to count on him, so I tried to keep what was happening under wraps. When we were together, I could almost pretend that everything was normal again, that my father was healthy and the biggest drama in my life was being thirty-two and single. Still, I had listened to Bob Dylan's "Sad-Eyed Lady of The Lowlands" a few thousand times too many and just longed for someone to see what was there in me.

Whenever my dad came up, he'd say, "I'm sorry I'm not good at consoling people." And then, "You're a good daughter."

The Thursday before Labor Day, Mark and I sat outside until it got dark, a bottle of bourbon between us. I was feeling a little sheepish about having picked a fight the week before.

"Do we need to talk about us?" I said.

"Do you *want* to talk about us?"

We'd had several versions of this conversation that summer.

When we'd started this up, he said, we'd been on the same page about not looking for anything. "What changed?" he asked.

I finally told the truth about my dad's cancer, which had spread from his pancreas to his liver, lungs, spleen—who knows where else? He'd decided not to pursue further treatment because there was nothing left to offer him.

I'd been thinking a lot about time, how we never know how much we have. I knew I wanted to be in a relationship, I said, so what was I doing spending time with someone who didn't want that with me? Technically, I could still be out there dating whomever I wanted, I admitted, but I just wasn't wired that way.

"We can do whatever you want," he said.

It had gotten dark a long time ago. Finally, Mark stood up to go inside and said, "Can I ask you something?"

By the look on his face, I thought he was going to ask me some kind of out-of-character deep question. I even allowed myself to imagine, for a split-second, that he might ask me if I wanted to start over, try that relationship thing.

"Could you . . . shave this for me?" He motioned to the nape of his neck.

My logic-brain knew that, like everything else about me, this was just a convenience for him—someone to reach a spot he couldn't— but my heart hooked onto this tiny, intimate moment, a glimmer of what I wanted. As the heavy razor hummed in my hand, I thought, how many times had I seen my mom do this for my dad? I wanted more moments like this, but in that bathroom with the too-bright lights, I realized this wasn't the place, the person.

I'd always found it strange that Mark called sex "making love" when he was so specific about how not "together" we were. It felt more like getting lost to me. That night though, it felt like the last leg of a long trip, when you're so past all sense of time and place, you almost forget where you've come from, where you're going. I just gave myself over to the quiet and the heat and forgot to worry about all the unknowns waiting for me. As we sat there on the couch afterwards, my ears rang. The city churned beyond the walls around us.

I didn't know it that night, but in a week's time I'd be shopping for a black dress. While sitting in a nail salon and writing the eulogy in Google Docs on my phone, I'd think to text Mark about the services. Part of me would want him there while part of me would worry about how to explain him to anyone.

What would I say to my family if he did come, I'd wonder? "Hey guys, this is Mark, the guy I'm 'hanging out with' because I don't want to be alone."

In the end, though, he would do the hard part for me. When I'd share the information for the wake, he'd say, "I'll try to swing by." Like it was a barbecue or something.

And suddenly, it would be so easy to let go.

But as we said goodnight that late August evening, I lingered a moment in the doorway, just taking him in, trying to lock in every detail. Something in me sensed the shift. Maybe we would still know each other after this, but I couldn't go back to "hanging out." Our kiss was drowsy, jet-lagged. I felt like I was on a transatlantic flight and unsure of the time zone, but I couldn't find the words to explain.

As I pulled away, I choked out, "I don't even know the depths of what I'm going through right now."

He nodded. It was barely a foot, but it felt like a quiet ocean between us. He made no move to cross. His stillness was all I needed to know.

I squeezed his hand goodbye and stepped out into the night.

END-OF-LIFE-CARE

CHAPTER 39

PLANNING FOR THE END OF LIFE

Suggested Listening: "A Dying Cubs Fan's Last Request"
—STEVE GOODMAN

In American culture, where we spend millions of dollars trying to stave off or deny aging, we also spend an incredible amount of energy avoiding the topic of death. While I credit my work in healthcare with helping me become at least a bit more comfortable acknowledging the inevitability of death, I still felt at a loss when it came to talking with my family about it. Sure, I wanted to help my dad have a good experience and be as comfortable as possible, and I knew my parents were having conversations throughout about arrangements, but it didn't feel like my business to bring it up.

When I was a kid, we used to listen to Steve Goodman's "A Dying Cub Fan's Last Request" a lot—I probably still know all the words—so sometimes we joked about hosting a Mets version for my dad, but my mom was the person he spoke with most about his wishes. He was clear about wanting a funeral and repast, and he wanted to be cremated, but at least with my sister and I, he didn't talk in great detail about what he envisioned for his death or what he thought might come next.

There are a lot of nuts-and-bolts types of things to consider, such as medical care for end of life, having plans in place for what to do in various situations that could arise, funeral arrangements, financial considerations, paperwork, figuring out what to do with social media accounts, and on and on. It can be an overwhelming and emotional process. Okay, not "can" be—it is. You're likely talking about things you never really thought you'd have to talk about. No one wants to think about this stuff. Regardless of whether or not you have an idea of how soon you may need to act on those plans, it's *a lot*.

I spoke with Alyssa Ackerman, a massage therapist and energy worker who is an end-of-life doula. She explained that she focuses on supporting conscious aging, dying, and grieving. When asked what an end-of-life doula (sometimes called a death doula) does, she said, "I am a nonmedical advocate who supports the dying person and their family. I offer somatic and spiritual care as well as planning and logistics through the process of dying and beyond."

In short, an end-of-life doula provides guidance and support through the process of dying.

On the practical side, death doulas may help with the process of defining and exploring the patient's advance directives and sharing those wishes with the patient's family so everyone can be on the same page and there is no confusion to complicate an already difficult time.

Another thing they can assist with is creating a legacy project before the person passes away. A legacy project is a physical project or activities you can do to honor the life of the person who is dying and share what they loved with those who come after. While someone doesn't have to be dying in order to create a legacy project (and it's recommended that we all consider our legacy long before we are dying), it can be a meaningful way to come together in someone's final days and beyond.

A death doula also holds loving and healing space for the person and their family, she added. "The dying person can feel very alone, and the family may be in denial of the approaching death. An end-of-life doula can help facilitate essential conversations that foster acceptance and great bonding through this time." Their work can also include things like meditation, guided visuals, breath work, massage, energy work (like Reiki), and more, depending on the doula. The doula may also offer respite care so the family can take a breath and tend to their own self-care needs.

"We also work on a vigil plan," Ackerman explained. "A vigil is the attentive watching through active dying. Doulas help a dying person and their family design the space and define their wishes for that time of active dying." For example, is there a particular way they want the room to look? Do they want candles? What music do they want to be playing? Who do they want to be there? It can be emotional to discuss but knowing that you are in service to the wishes of your loved one can be healing through one's process of saying goodbye.

Of course, you obviously don't need to work with a death doula, but they are an incredible resource for those facing advanced illness and death. They are an advocate for the family and the dying person. They can offer incredible peace and support so the family / loved ones can come together in this time. Ackerman recommends asking your doctor or other healthcare providers you work with such as a massage therapist or acupuncturist for recommendations. The palliative care department of a hospital or healthcare center can be another valuable resource when looking for an end-of-life doula. For those interested in learning more or connecting with a doula, she recommends using her directory at www.soulfulsenescence.com to find a doula near them.

CHAPTER 40

HAVE THE DIFFICULT CONVERSATIONS

Suggested Listening: "Leaving on a Jet Plane"
—JOHN DENVER

I'm not usually one for regrets, but sometimes I do look back and wish I had asked more questions. When my father was dying, I think I was so fixated on the tasks in front of me, I had a hard time slowing down enough to hear my own heart and acknowledge what I'd later want answers to.

In part, I felt shy about asking. On another level, I also sensed my dad's resistance. He was an emotional guy, but he expressed his feelings on his terms. I didn't always feel comfortable bringing up heavier topics—I didn't want to make him upset or ruin a good day he might be having. I wanted to ask him questions about his life and what brought him joy, but I also wanted to ask him about his fears, what he thought about death.

I asked Ackerman about navigating these difficult conversations. The fears people have around death, she said, depend on the stage in their process. "I hear a lot of people who are not terminal but aging and are thinking and talking about their wishes. They fear becoming a burden to the family. It often breaks down to the fear of losing dignity and consuming energy and resources. These end-of-life stages are asking something totally different of us than our productive and family rearing stages, but our culture does not take this into consideration."

She added, "We often idealize the young, productive, and independent, instead of honoring our elders and flowing with the change of pace that elderhood asks and requires of us. For those who are concerned about becoming a burden, it is key to remember how good it feels to help and to give. If you never receive care, help, or support from others, we are refusing the love of others and we are preventing a deeper connection. The best thing those who are worried about becoming a burden can do is to make plans now."·

Another thing she shared that comes up a lot in her work is that there is significant fear around being forgotten. "I see that related to a lack of ritual around remembering our ancestors that connects them to their beloved deceased. There is great fear of being forgotten, being erased, being deleted, or disappearing. I work with folks to rewrite this, create ritual, to integrate the memory of our dead into our lives."

"Being in pain is another big fear. Though hospice does a great job of providing comfort from physical pain, medication doesn't really touch spiritual pain in someone who is dying. It's important to acknowledge, validate, and to be with them through the fear of spiritual pain, and this is a place where a death doula, or a spiritual leader/friend can come in to support. Simple conversations from family and friends can help soothe that fear and anxiety."

How to Have Those Conversations

I spoke with Karen Noé, a renowned psychic medium, spiritual counselor, and healer with a two-year waiting list, about having those difficult conversations with a loved one who is on a difficult health journey. She is the Hay House author of *We Conscious-*

ness: 33 Profound Truths for Inner and Outer Peace, Your Life After Their Death: A Medium's Guide to Healing After a Loss, Through the Eyes of Another: A Medium's Guide to Creating Heaven on Earth by Encountering Your Life Review Now, and The Rainbow Follows the Storm: How to Obtain Inner Peace by Connecting with Angels and Deceased Loved Ones.

"You need to ask the person what they feel comfortable talking about," she said. "For example, if they are terminal and ready to go, they may wish to talk about what they believe is on the other side. On the other hand, if they desire to stay, then they probably wish to talk about what they can do to get well." She always reminds people (patients and caregivers alike) to be mindful of the words they use. "Make sure to use positive words when you speak to them. Use words that make them feel comfortable," she added.

When talking with them about death, she said, "If you're a caregiver for someone who is ready to pass, it's important to leave it up to them. Ask them what they want to do. It's okay if they say they're tired. They're not wrong if they decide they don't want to fight anymore. They need to know that. You just need to give them permission and stand by their side."

For someone who is ready to pass, she recommends having them watch programs about near-death experiences. One such show is Life to Afterlife and Back, where people talk about their near-death experiences and how peaceful it is on the other side. I would ask them if there is anything about these programs they would like to discuss. This is a good opportunity for them to make peace and heal.

In Through the Eyes of Another, Noé writes about how it is beneficial to go through a life review before one passes. So many times, those who have gone through a near-death experience talk about things they've encountered on "the other side," including seeing through each person's eyes how they've affected them.

They also talk about now being able to understand certain things they *could have* or *should have* done differently. Many times, it's as simple as realizing they should have told their loved ones just how much they meant to them.

"So, why do we have to wait until we die to see through the other person's eyes? We can do it now and create peace in our lives and in their lives as well." She shared this story about her experience with her mother:

"In this book, I talk about writing letters to our significant loved ones, telling them how much we love them. I had written one to my mom before she was sick, telling her how much she meant to me and the reasons why I was proud of her. A year later, she became terminally ill and was in a coma. When I went to visit her at her home, I saw the letter I had written on her desk and decided to read it to her. As I did, tears began flowing down her face. She heard what I was saying, even though she was in a coma.

"I recommend writing your loved ones this type of letter. Talk about how much you love them and how they made a difference in your life. If there is a need for forgiveness, tell them you forgive them or give them a chance to forgive you."

If you're feeling stumped over how to initiate those conversations (or knowing when to hold back) her advice is to watch your loved one's reaction. "You sit with them and say, 'Do you want to talk?' They'll say 'no' or they'll say, 'Yeah, I do.' Allow them to discuss whatever they feel is important. They may need to vent. It's easier said than done to just listen, but it's important to let them get it all out."

Clinical Social Worker Lauren Langford has helped countless patients and families navigate these conversations. "It's best to start with normalizing it. Every one of us has to die. It's a part of the life cycle. You're in a powerful position that you know you're going to pass away, and you can be in control over what you'd like this to look like. Really empower the person to make their own end-of-life decisions. What do they envision their death to look like? Who would they like to be there? Where would they like it to be? What kind of life celebration would they hope for? When you empower people, they are more on board with it." She also encourages bringing religious beliefs and spirituality into it if that is a part of that person's life.

"I also think it's about meeting the person where they're at. If they're not ready to have that conversation, they're not ready. That's their right. And sometimes it's a process for people. They have to get used to the diagnosis and, later, that things are not going well. I have noticed that for people with a terminal illness, it does crystalize eventually."

Lauren Chiarello, whom I interviewed about making movement a part of your life when you're a caregiver, also had some insight into this area. She has a unique perspective from having gone through cancer treatment twice and then, later, caring for her twin infant sons while one was in the hospital for the first months of his life.

When I asked her about what things it may be helpful for caregivers to say (or not say) to someone going through treatment, she said, "This is where active listening really comes in. It certainly depends on the person and their personality. Listening is so important. Oftentimes, when we're in a caregiver situation, we just want to fix it all. A lot of times, it's really about just holding space for the person. We may want to just jump in and make everything better, but sometimes holding back a little is important. When I was going through treatment, I really wanted to be heard and seen and get my feelings out there and have that be okay." For the person who is being cared for, "It's important to feel your feelings and have that acceptance."

She added that is incredibly meaningful when caregivers "can do the deep listening and just hold the space, offering messages like, 'I hear you, I'm with you, I'm walking with you. Let me know if you need anything. I'm showing up, I'm ready.' Knowing you have someone you can count on is meaningful when you're navigating a life hurdle. Knowing you have people in your life that will show up for you in the bright as well as the dark moment is so meaningful."

If you're worried about not knowing what to say, she recommends letting go of that hang-up. "You might not have all the right things to say or even anything to say, but the practice of showing up is huge."

CHAPTER 41

WITHOUT-A-DOUBT SIGNS

Suggested Listening: "Ripple"
— G R A T E F U L   D E A D

A few chapters ago I told you the origin story about how my thing with feathers officially became A Thing. To this day, when I find a feather in an unusual place or something about it stands out to me in a way it wouldn't normally, it feels like what Karen Noé calls a "without-a-doubt sign": a sign from someone who has passed.

Sure, things like feathers and coins in your path can be signs (and Noé recommends you save these when you find them), but a "without-a-doubt sign" tends to be very personal or something that wouldn't normally happen—something that's impossible to write off or ignore.

"After they pass, you could ask them to give you a without-a-doubt sign."

She said that our deceased loved ones like to communicate with us through animals. "They're able to use their energy to go into an animal and the animal would do something it normally wouldn't do, something that stands out."

She also said to watch out for interesting electrical happenings.

"They also love to play with electricity, close and open garage doors, or make the lights go on and off."

Numbers are another common sign. "They like to show you the same numbers or sequences of numbers enough to get your attention."

Music can also be a way you may get a without-a-doubt sign. "They give you a specific song with the words you need to hear at the perfect time" or a song that you associate with them.

She also says to pay attention to your dreams. "They love to come to us in dreams. You need to wake up after the dream in order to remember it." There is a difference, she explained, between a true visitation and a dream from your subconscious where you are worrying about them. "If you dream about your grandfather in the casket and he's mad at you, that's your subconscious. If it feels good, it's usually a true visitation. A real visitation will feel great. A dream from your subconscious will feel scary or stressful."

My mother says my dad appears to her as a dragonfly. To my sister, it's as a blue jay. Of course, I think of my dad when I see feathers, but he comes to me in dreams sometimes too. Because music was such a part of our life as a family, sometimes when certain songs come on it can resonate like a sign as well.

CHAPTER 42

THE FAREWELL TOUR

Suggested Listening: "Rocket Man"
—ELTON JOHN

I got to the house on Friday night, hungover and furiously scratching at mosquito bites that had bloomed after my evening with Mark. My dad was so delirious and out of breath he couldn't even stand up. He wouldn't eat. He was amenable to trying red Jello when it was offered, but it just fell out of his mouth onto the bedspread. By Saturday morning, it was clear that this was more than just needing fluids.

My mom called a car service and we packed a bag for him while he sat on the stairs, too weak to move. Even though it was late August and blazing hot, my dad was always cold now, and I knew that it would feel extra icy in the hospital air conditioning, so I threw in a pair of cozy socks.

On the drive into the city, I sat in the backseat with him, holding his hand. He thought it was Easter and kept asking what time we were meeting the family for dinner. Somehow, I kept a neutral face. Of course, I was terrified, but the fact that he was so fixated on Easter was also deeply funny to me. He'd always *hated* Easter celebrations with my extended family! This made it even more clear that something was off, even if he *was* The New

Catholic. We called my sister and her husband, who were about to start their Labor Day weekend off at the beach, and told them to turn around.

Because a holiday weekend is basically the worst time to seek medical care, we ended up waiting for hours in the hallway of MSK's Urgent Care until he could be seen. I went out every few hours to get my mom food and coffee. Having worked on that block for almost five years, I knew where the good spots were, and I'll be honest, it did me a lot of good to walk around a familiar neighborhood where I had memories of feeling like a functional, capable human who could solve my patients' problems.

When he finally got into a bed to start fluids and a blood transfusion. My mom put the socks I'd packed on his feet. He looked at me and grinned. "We are so lucky your mother is here."

He told my sister over the phone that he was getting fluids and then was going to get on a plane. By the time he was admitted to the hospital we had been in the Urgent Care for almost twenty-four hours. As it turned out, he had severe internal bleeding and some kind of bacterial infection. His body was exhausted.

Over the course of the long weekend, I bit my lower lip to keep from crying as I looked at the labs that popped up in the patient portal app my mom stalked on her phone. I don't know what's harder: not knowing what those numbers mean or knowing exactly what they mean and not being able to do anything about it. My dad never did anything half-assed, so we sampled just about every specialty service they had: obviously, oncology, but also urology, liver, heme, cardiac, neuro . . .

Ever the showman, somehow, he kept us laughing the whole time. When the neurologist came to evaluate him, she asked him what month it was, what year. He wasn't sure about either of those, but when she asked him who the president was, he knew right away. "Unfortunately, Donald Trump."

He must have screened in for weight loss (about forty pounds) because at some point a dietitian came by to ask my dad if he wanted a milkshake, which, in a hospital, is really just lactose-free goop in a can. By this point, though, his labs were trending in the direction of WELL, FUCK THIS. I wanted to say something snarky to her, but I also knew that this woman was just doing her job. How many times had I been her?

Labor Day morning, my dad had a small heart attack. If you've ever been in a hospital and had chest pain or been with someone who has, then you know that about twenty people show up in your room, asking you questions and sticking things on and in your body.

And of course, my dad just *had* to let the rapid response team know that I was single. He knew *of* Mark but was not a big fan of the situation.

Later that day I teased him. "Really, Dad? Was that really necessary?"

"How could I be in a room full of hot doctors and *not* mention it? Besides, I've always wanted a doctor for a son-in-law."

There was one doctor in particular that weekend who my dad had his eye on for me, one who spent a lot of time with us while he watched my dad to make sure he didn't go into cardiac arrest before they could transfer him to the ICU. He was really pleasant and funny, and I kept meaning to write down his name, but there was so much going on, I forgot. In retrospect, I'm glad I didn't.

Monday night, Labor Day, some friends came to visit and we just tried to enjoy this last encore of my dad's energy. That night, though, he started to deteriorate. My sister's husband took her home, but I stayed late. Around 9:00 pm I finally went out to grab my mom some food and toiletries so she could spend the night in his room. I was hesitant to go, knowing this might be the last chance I'd get to have a conversation with my dad. I knelt down to kiss his cheek and told him I loved him.

His voice was tired but clear. "I love you too."

The next morning, he had another cardiac event and was having so much trouble breathing he had to be sedated and intubated. I got in a cab as soon as my mom texted me. When I got to the hospital, my clinical brain switched on so I could stay calm and walk her through the steps to make it seem like just some everyday procedure, but when I checked his newest labs, I burst into tears.

They moved him to the ICU as soon as a bed became available and explained that there was nothing they could do. Any one of the things he had going on could have kept him on life support for weeks at a time with no hope of actual recovery. As the doctor's mouth moved, I felt like I was back in school, worried I was about to be called on when I wasn't ready. Fortunately, the actual decision-making process that morning was simple. Because my parents had talked about my dad's wishes, it was agreed that after his sister got there and we all had some time to say goodbye, we would turn off the respirator.

The hospital staff was amazing. They made sure my dad was comfortable and when they found out about how much he loved music, they encouraged us to plug his phone into the USB speakers. So yeah, we were that family blasting classic rock in the ICU.

Around one o'clock, I went to grab my mom some food, and when I came back into the dim room, Elton John's "Rocket Man" was blaring.

My eyes welled up. "I love this song," I said. I sat down in the empty chair next to her and just listened.

Around six, after my aunt had arrived and we'd all gotten to spend some time together with my dad, the nurse asked my mom if she wanted any religious services. It wasn't long before a priest walked into the room. My aunt got one look at his robes and the Bible tucked under his arm and said, "Who the hell invited *him?*""

My mother said, "Uh, I did. Your brother's a Catholic now." I bit my lip to keep from laughing.

My aunt shrugged. "Well, I guess I kind of am too—by marriage, anyway."

So we prayed together. None of us were particularly religious, but it was actually so much simpler than I'd realized—it was about love and just being there around my dad's bedside. I could never unknow that now.

It began to get dark. The nurse came back in and my mom must have been the one to say it was time. So we turned off the machines and just . . . waited.

INTERVIEW WITH
WILLIE NILE

Suggested Listening: "One Guitar"
—WILLIE NILE

E ven though they had worked together for decades, the first
time I actually met American singer-songwriter Willie Nile
in person was at my dad's wake. The service itself was a bit of
a who's who in 80s and 90s rock radio history. The funny thing
about the music industry is the hair, for the men, especially. Either
they have no hair, or, like, a big head of rock'n'roll hair. There's
a certain clothing style too—a lot of black even when nobody's
died.

I was feeling kind of jealous that day of my mom and sister,
who had already found feathers in their path—from my dad, they
said. But I was the one with the feather thing! I felt immature for
caring, but I couldn't help it.

Then in walked Willie Nile (Team Hair), wearing a necklace
with a giant feather dangling from it.

Because I am my father's daughter, unless I'm actively trying
not to put my foot in my mouth, I have no filter. "We've never
met," I said, "but I saw your necklace and I have to tell you something about feathers."

He was kind enough to listen to my story and tell me one about when his mother passed. When I interviewed him about it for this book several years later, he said, "When you told me that about the feather, and I was wearing this necklace, I loved that. I take those things in a positive light. I see them as messages, signs, and things with a good spin on them. My mother died at 87 years old, an only child. She had eight children. She died at home in a hospital bed, surrounded by her kids and grandkids. Two or three days later there was this huge thunderstorm, and lightning struck by the sidewalk outside their window and the grass was burned halfway toward the window. I said, 'Dad, that's a sign. That's Mom saying, Hey.'"

Paraphrasing Shakespeare's *Hamlet*, he added, "*There are more things between heaven and earth than are dreamt of in your philosophies.*" We talked about feeling like your loved ones are still around. "When my mother died, some things happened that were not 'normal'— I still feel her around and her love coming at me." While not everyone has a religious grounding, he added, "My parents' faith served them well. You treat people well, do the best you can, and leave the rest in God's hands. Why limit the possibilities?

"I loved and respected your dad. He was a solid cat and a friend for life. He meant it. He was no phony. He was the real deal. He was a man of the world who saw the good, the bad, and the ugly and pursued his passion—music, he had that kind of wisdom."

When I started working on this book, I knew I wanted to speak with him about his many years of experience on the road. Here, Nile, who has been called "a one-man Clash" and the creator of many acclaimed albums, answers my questions.

What are some of the physical health challenges that come up with touring?

When I first started out, I'd be burning the candle at both ends and soon enough realized I had to take better care if I wanted to survive and continue making music, which, fortunately I've done. Of course, you have the normal ones of fatigue from the travel when it's long hours. I take pretty good care of myself so I've been pretty lucky and can deal with it. I did have to learn, though.

In 1980 my band and I did a three-week tour and ended up in LA. The Who's management people came backstage one night. The Who had already started a tour and the management asked me to open for them across the country. Next thing I know, I'm playing for thousands of people in arenas. It was a total blast, but I had never toured like that before and was exhausted because we would play a half-hour set and then watch The Who show, party, drink, go to bed, carry on. And I had to wake up early. Because I was this new artist, I had to do interviews and be on the phone all day in my hotel room. Then we'd do sound check, eat, play, watch The Who . . . a few weeks of that.

I had the time of my life but was so overworked on tour. The demands on my body, lack of sleep, alcohol, I think there was cocaine around on that tour. I never did a lot of that, but what I did didn't do me any good. Something in me snapped.

One night in July, we were in Georgia. It was really hot. Earlier that day, when my road manager and I had been coming back up from an interview, we'd gotten stuck in an elevator with about twenty people. Fortunately, it opened up soon, but when I was sitting in the back of the plane later, I felt like, "I have to get out of here." I asked the flight attendant, Can I get off? I walked twenty feet away from the plane to just get some air. I went back on, sat down, and was so claustrophobic.

I eventually got over it, but for some years after, my claustrophobia was so bad, I could barely get on a plane or go into buildings. All I could think was, "I've got to get out of here."

There are lots of good things about being on tour, though. Your father knew this—at the end of the day, it's a good workout and can border on ecstasy. It's a celebration.

I always try to take good care of myself. If I get enough sleep most things are easy enough to deal with.

What are some of the emotional and mental health challenges?

Family and close friends, that's what it's all about. Whether that's people you grow up with or people you meet along the way on the road. On tour, you see people you don't get to see a lot. Sometimes the distance away from home can be wearing, though. I walked away from the business after my second album because I didn't want the business end of things to spoil my buzz for music. When it became more about business than music, I stopped touring for the rest of the 80s other than one show in Norway.

I wasn't a road dog for years and years. I'm a poet. The heaviest touring I've done has been in the last ten to fifteen years. Because I'm older, I can measure it and pace myself. I think the music keeps me younger. I think that's a key. I'm still writing and putting out records. Maybe because I'm older, I can handle it better. I believe there can be salvation and healing from music. My band and I are very close. We're family. When we're out on the road together we share the ups and the downs, the good and the bad, and the bond it creates is mighty. It's a brotherhood to be treasured.

When I started out, I just wanted to write songs about things I cared about, make a living, take care of my family. I never thought fame was something that would get me to any place worth getting to. When I'm touring, the music heals me every night.

Is there anything you wish you had known about how to take care of yourself on the road when you were just starting out?
If I had any advice to give I'd just say to believe in yourself. Be open. Follow your dreams. You never know where they'll take you. Try to get people around you that you can trust who have your best interests at heart. Give it all you've got. Trust your gut, trust your instincts. And don't take No for answer.

Do you travel with a bag of essentials?
When I travel, I do have a small bag with some essential things like keys, fluids, things to read, pens, paper, phone, snacks, lyrics I'm working on, that sort of thing.

CHAPTER 43

AFTER THE SHOW

Suggested Listening: "Thunder Road"
(Live at the Roxy Theatre, 1975)
—BRUCE SPRINGSTEEN

"Wish You Were Here"
—PINK FLOYD

I am not the person to write a grief book, but the most helpful pieces of advice I was given were, "Grief is not linear" and "The only way is through."

Holistic psychiatrist Ellen Vora shared that, when you're going through grief, sleep and crying are good things to prioritize. "Sleep is this magical space that heals and recharges us. It's also when our unconscious does our best processing of what we're going through. Dreaming is when I reconnect with my mom since she passed. So I would say prioritize sleep above everything else."

We're a culture that rewards stoicism and productivity and smiling through the tough times, so it's not uncommon to find yourself apologizing for crying or to berate yourself for crying when you should be doing something else. "We think crying is somehow a bad thing and we apologize and try to suck it back in and make it small. We seem to be conditioned to be strong and not cry, but I think there is a different form of strong," she says. "Crying is quintessentially human. It helps us de-stress, release, and bond. We need to build it into our schedules. Sometimes it has to happen on its own schedule. It sometimes comes up at unexpected moments. We are such a productivity-obsessed culture, but this is your *life*, and tears of grief are here to honor your connections and the people you love."

She adds that it's better to share your grief with others than trying to keep it under wraps or shield others in your life from it. "When my mom passed away, my husband grieved with me. When I would cry, he would cry. It really helped my grieving process. It needs to be witnessed. The wave needs to get to full crest, where nobody is apologizing or trying to bring it back in. It needs to be fully expressed. I loved that he was feeling it with me and going through it and it allowed me to have a very complete grieving experience."

Grief can be a time to lean into and explore your individual spirituality, she says. "It depends on who you are, but we're all in these different phases, on a different curve in relation to our belief in something. Some people are just raised with it and it's working for them and are grooving with it, and some others are in a rebellion against organized religion. Especially around grief and caretaking, it's worth exploring your spirituality and your feelings about it. What feels true to you? I wasn't raised religious and actually had to rebel against *that* and connect to something that felt true to me. I found immense meaning and comfort in that when I lost my mom. Wherever you are on that rebellion or acceptance curve, reexamine it and explore what feels true to you."

For the first few weeks, all I wanted to do was clean. I organized every drawer, purged countless items from my closets and cabinets. Even though I was still relying on recipe development and content creation for a lot of my income, the last thing I wanted to do was cook. I ate a lot of salad and sardines and yogurt.

While I tried to process what I could, I also dove headfirst into writing *The Little Book of Game Changers*, banging out a

60,000-word manuscript in 90 days. I somehow also had more clients and projects than ever before. My mom and sister lightened their workloads where they could, but I was focusing so hard on my business, it seemed, at first, that I had learned nothing. I would go out to events or write all day or see clients and then come home, meditate, write some more . . .

I suddenly loathed New York and its crowded spaces, I got it into my head that I was going to move to California. In retrospect, I think I was just tired—I just hadn't been able to feel it before because we'd been going at such a grueling pace with my dad. But when was I going to finally let myself rest? Did I even *know* how to rest in the city?

The Farewell Tour was over, and I didn't like what I had left to come home to. Having been around my dad's big personality so much over the past fifteen months and seen what a rich life he had had, it highlighted how much of that richness I lacked. On paper, it seemed I had accomplished quite a bit since leaving home at nineteen, but when it came to my personal life, standing there again in my studio apartment with my suitcase fully unpacked this time, it was hard to ignore how small I had made my own life.

I started by taking driving lessons, since I'd barely been behind the wheel in fifteen years. Then I signed up for a storytelling class to get me out of the apartment on Monday nights. I also changed therapists. I started dating again a little earlier than planned and actually enjoyed it this time. In my head, I was moving, anyway, so why not have a little fun? But then, something funny happened: I realized it wasn't New York that was the problem. My feelings of closed-off-ness would have followed me across the country. I decided to open myself up to whatever I was at the beginning of.

I slowly got interested in cooking again. It was the sudden desire to make a pot of marinara that finally brought me back. My mother's recipe. As the familiar smell wafted through my tiny apartment, Bruce Springsteen's "Thunder Road" came through the speakers, and I found myself laughing and crying at the same time, wooden spoon in hand. The ice around me was starting to crack and fall away.

What Dr. Vora says about sleep and dreaming as a way of connecting with a loved one really resonates with me. My dad sometimes comes to me in my dreams. The ones where I wake up knowing it was a visitation are usually strange and funny and sweet, and he usually has a very specific message to share or something he wants to show me.

The first dream I ever had like this was a few months after he'd died, the night after my first date with the man I'd end up marrying. It wasn't even on my radar that this handsome Midwesterner was my person—I had *no* idea what to do with someone who was attractive, confident, *and* kind. Was that really a thing? Besides, I was planning to move to California the next month. Still, as I rode the subway home that night, something in my gut told me that I would know him, I just didn't know what that meant yet.

That night I dreamt I was standing on a street corner waiting for the light to change when I felt my phone vibrate. I pulled it out and saw my dad's number on the caller ID.

"Dad?"

"Don't hang up," he said. "It's really me. I can do this now."

I said I loved him and missed him. We talked for a minute and then he got to the point. "So," he said.

"So."

"I really like this one."

The light turned green, and I woke up.

THE FAREWELL
TOUR PLAYLIST

"End of The Line"—Traveling Wilburys
"I'm From New Jersey"—John Gorka
"Teach Your Children"—Crosby, Stills, Nash & Young
"New Amsterdam"—Elvis Costello and the Attractions
"It's Only Rock & Roll (But I Like It)"—The Rolling Stones
"Sleep On Needles"—Sondre Lerche
"A Shot in the Arm"—Wilco
"Space Oddity"—David Bowie
"I Need Never Get Old"—Nathaniel Rateliff & the Night Sweats
"Marie Provost"—Nick Lowe
"Changes"—Langhorne Slim & the Law
"Pink Houses"—John Mellencamp
"I Won't Back Down" –Johnny Cash
"Chicken Cordon Bleus (Live)"—Steve Goodman
"Welcome To The Working Week"—Elvis Costello
"Sisters of Mercy"—Leonard Cohen
"Handle With Care"—Jenny Lewis and the Watson Twins
"Not Fade Away"—The Rolling Stones
"Burned"—Buffalo Springfield

"Where Is My Mind?"—Pixies
"I Ain't the Same"—Alabama Shakes
"Watching the Wheels (acoustic)"—John Lennon
"(What's So Funny 'Bout) Peace, Love, and Understanding?"
    —Nick Lowe
"Cure For Pain"—Morphine
"Waltz About Whiskey"—Watchhouse
"Swept Away"—Avett Brothers
"And Your Bird Can Sing (Take 2 / Anthology 2 Version)"
    —The Beatles
"Rise"—Eddie Vedder
"Coming In to Los Angeles"—Sarah Lee Guthrie
"Head Underwater"—Jenny Lewis
"Even the Darkness has Arms"—Barr Brothers
"The Sound of Silence (Acoustic)"—Simon & Garfunkel
"A Whiter Shade of Pale"—Procol Harum
"Hands Together"—Scratch Track
"These Days (Live)"—Jackson Browne
"Mona Lisas and Mad Hatters"—Elton John
"What Light"—Wilco
"Starman"—David Bowie
"Still Not Dead"—Willie Nelson
"Small Town Moon"—Regina Spektor
"I'll Be Here in the Morning"—Townes Van Zandt
"Wild Wide Open Spaces (Live)"—Whiskey Treaty Roadshow
"American Without Tears"—Elvis Costello
"Birds (Live at the Cellar Door)"—Neil Young
"White Winter Hymnal"—Fleet Foxes
"Rivers and Roads"—The Head and The Heart
"All Your Favorite Bands"—Dawes
"Turn! Turn! Turn! (To Everything There Is a Season)"
    —The Byrds

"All I Really Want to Do (Live at Philharmonic Hall, New York, NY Oct 1964)"—Bob Dylan

"Tell Me Why"—Neil Young

"Goodmorning"—Bleachers

"A Dying Cubs Fan's Last Request"—Steve Goodman

"Leaving on a Jet Plane"—John Denver

"Ripple"—Grateful Dead

"Rocket Man (I Think It's Gonna Be a Long, Long Time)"—Elton John

"One Guitar"—Willie Nile

"Thunder Road (Live at the Roxy Theatre 1975)"—Bruce Springsteen

"Wish You Were Here"—Pink Floyd"

The Farewell Tour book playlist is available on Spotify.

SELF-CARE FOR CAREGIVERS CHEAT SHEET

NUTRITION

- Balance your blood sugar with a combo of protein, fat, and fiber at meals and snacks

- Make it convenient to eat well; plan what you can

- Embrace healthy shortcuts

- Don't ignore cravings—get curious about them!

- Drink plenty of water and be careful not to overdo caffeine or alcobol.

MOVEMENT

- Something is better than nothing

- Do what feels good and fits into your lifestyle

- Don't compare yourself to others

- Use movement to shift your energy and process emotions

- More is not always better; don't overdo it and burn out

STRESS

- Stress has physical, mental, and emotional health effects

- Fix what you can

- Make a stress management plan with support from others

- Watch out for caregiver burnout

- Eating balanced meals, moving our body, and getting enough rest can all help with stress management

ORGANIZATION

- Use a calendar to track appointments, payment deadlines, prescription refills, and other relevant information

- Store paperwork and other items in a safe space you can easily access

- Delegate tasks if needed

- Set boundaries with your time and energy

RELATIONSHIPS

- Accept that your relationships will change

- Ask for what you need

If you're dating, be clear about what you are looking for

- Set clear boundaries

- Surround yourself with people who uplift you

SPIRITUALITY

- Reflect on the role spirituality has (or has not) played in your life

- Explore what resonates with you

- Spend time in meditation or prayer or in nature

ACKNOWLEDGMENTS

There are so many people I want to thank for helping me bring this book out into the world:

First off, I want to thank my family for their emotional support and shared memories, for being on the journey with me.

And all my love to my husband Jacob, who has met Writing Cave Jess and chose to stay married to us. I always appreciate your willingness to talk through whatever it is I need to talk through.

I also want to thank my agent, the wonderful Leigh Eisenman. Thanks for talking me out of the oracle cards thing—this was a much better way to spend my energy.

My deepest gratitude to the incredible team at Viva Editions: especially Rene Sears, Ashley Calvano, and Meghan Kilduff for working so closely with me on this project. Special thanks to Heather Huzovic for helping us get the word out.

I also want to acknowledge Jade Dressler, Paulina Kajankova, Francesca Latham, Melissa Ingle, and Heather Piedmont for keeping me organized behind the scenes.

I am so appreciative of all the health experts, music industry professionals, and artists, who shared their stories and expertise with me. And thank you to Allyssa Fortunato and Rebecca Shapiro for your warmth, generosity, and your insight as I was developing this project.

In addition, I want to thank my colleagues as well as my past and current patients and clients—you've taught me so much.

Also, to Adam Wade, whose storytelling class was the first place I ever talked about *The Farewell Tour* experience, thank you for giving me a safe place to find my voice again.

This book was written during the COVID-19 pandemic, when I was getting used to a totally new phase of my personal and professional life and getting reacquainted with the sound of my own heart again after being constantly on the go and surrounded by noise for years. The prayer every day was the same: *Show me what to do next.*

The week I sat down to write these acknowledgments, my father came to me in a dream. I was on vacation doing yoga (like I said, a dream); and he showed up wearing a shirt that said, "Do what you love, love what you live" on it. He smiled and explained he'd waited to visit until I was quiet and calm and could actually hear and see him.

A lot of this book came to me in dreams. I would go to bed asking for guidance—on who to reach out to for an interview or how to structure a particular section, or which part of a story to share and which to leave out—and I'd wake up with a solution to jot down in the notebook next to my bed. At other times I got unexpected ideas and insights while asleep.

The entire idea of interviewing any musicians at all began that way, from a dream where I ran into an artist who'd worked with my dad for many years, and we sat down and had a conversation about my father. When I woke up, I turned to my husband and said, "I have this crazy idea that's going to make this project even more complicated, but I know I need to follow this thread."

I wrote most of this book sitting cross-legged on my old bed in my parents' house. I am eternally grateful to my mother for giving my husband and I a place to live while we were between homes after relocating for my work. It had not been part of the plan to write about my own history in the place where I'd lived so much of it, but for whatever reason, it was supposed to be that way. I know I'll look back and be happy I got to spend the time with her, sharing memories, thoughts, and stories on our morning walks.

ENDNOTES

1   American Psychological Association. Stress Effects on the Body. Accessed online February 5 2021. https://www.apa.org/topics/stress/body

2   The Mayo Clinic. Stress Symptoms: Effects on Your Body and Behavior. Accessed online February 7 2021. https://www.mayoclinic.org/healthy-lifestyle/stress-management/in-depth/stress-symptoms/art-20050987

3   Cleveland Clinic. Caregiver Burnout. Accessed online February 12 2021. https://my.clevelandclinic.org/health/diseases/9225-caregiver-burnout

4   Obesity Medicine Association. Obesity and Insulin Resistance. Accessed online February 27 2021. https://obesitymedicine.org/obesity-and-insulin-resistance/

5   American Diabetes Association. Understanding A1c. Accessed online February 27 2021. https://www.diabetes.org/a1c

6   Wang X, Lin X, Ouyang YY, Liu J, Zhao G, Pan A, Hu FB. Red and Processed Meat Consumption and Mortality: Dose-Response Meta-Analysis of Prospective Cohort Studies. *Public Health Nutr.* 2016 April: 19(5):893–905. doi: 10.1017/S1368980015002062. Epub 2015 Jul 6. PMID: 26143683. Accessed online September 25 2021. https://pubmed.ncbi.nlm.nih.gov/26143683/

7   John B. Furness, Brid P. Callaghan, Leni R. Rivera, and Hyun-Jung Cho. The Enteric Nervous System and Gastrointestinal Innervation: Integrated Local and Central Control. *Adv Exp Med Biol.* 2014 817:

39–71. Accessed online March 6 2021. https://pubmed.ncbi.nlm.nih .gov/24997029/

8   Candace Fung and Pieter Vanden Berghe. Functional Circuits and Signal Processing in the Enteric Nervous System. *Cellular and Molecular Life Sciences.* 2020 77:4505–4522. Accessed online March 6 2021. https:// link.springer.com/article/10.1007/s00018-020-03543-6

9   Patterson E, Wall R, Fitzgerald GF, Ross RP, Stanton C. Health Implications of High Dietary Omega-6 Polyunsaturated Fatty Acids. *J Nutr Metab.* 2012: 539426. doi: 10.1155/2012/539426. Epub 2012 April 5. PMID: 22570770; PMCID: PMC3335257. Accessed online September 25 2021. https://pubmed.ncbi.nlm.nih.gov/22570770/

10 Vitamin D Fact Sheet For Health Professionals. National Institutes of Health Office of Dietary Supplements. Accessed online April 29 2021. https://ods.od.nih.gov/factsheets/VitaminD-HealthProfessional/

11 Qin Xiang Ng , Shawn Shao Hong Koh, Hwei Wuen Chan, Collin Yih Xian Ho, Clinical Uses of Curcumin in Depression: A Meta-Analysis. *J Am Med Dir Assoc.* 2017 June 1 18(6): 503–508. Accessed Online May 8 2021. https://pubmed.ncbi.nlm.nih.gov/28236605/

12 National Institutes of Health. Omega-3 Fatty Acids Fact Sheet for Health Professionals. Accessed online September 26 2021. https://ods .od.nih.gov/factsheets/Omega3FattyAcids-HealthProfessional/

13 Boyle NB, Lawton C, Dye L. The Effects of Magnesium Supplementation on Subjective Anxiety and Stress—A Systematic Review. *Nutrients.* 2017 9(5): 429. https://doi.org/10.3390/nu9050429

14 National Institues of Health. Probiotics Fact Sheet For Health Professionals. Accessed online August 20 2021. https://ods.od.nih.gov/ factsheets/Probiotics-HealthProfessional/

15 Aguilar-Toalá JE, Garcia-Varela R, Garcia HS, et al. Postbiotics: An Evolving Term Within the Functional Foods Field. Trends Food Sci Tech. 2018 75: 105–114.

16 Sanlier N, Gökcen BB, Sezgin AC. Health Benefits of Fermented Foods. Crit Rev Food Sci Nutr. 2019 59(3): 506–527.

17 Thomas Larrieu and Sophie Layé. Food for Mood: Relevance of nutritional omega-3 fatty acids for depression and anxiety. *Front Physiol.* 2018 9: 1047. Accessed online March 21 2021. https://www .ncbi.nlm.nih.gov/pmc/articles/PMC6087749/

18 Vitamin D Fact Sheet For Health Professionals. National Institutes of Health Office of Dietary Supplements. Accessed online March 20 2021.

https://ods.od.nih.gov/factsheets/VitaminD-HealthProfessional/

19 Gabriela Marcelino, Priscila Aiko Hiane, Karine de Cássia Freitas, Lidiani Figueiredo Santana, Arnildo Pott, Juliana Rodrigues Donadon, Rita de Cássia Avellaneda Guimarães. Effects of Olive Oil and Its Minor Components on Cardiovascular Diseases, Inflammation, and Gut Microbiota. *Nutrients.* 2019 August 11(8): 1826. Accessed online March 20 2021. https://www.ncbi.nlm.nih.gov/pmc/articles/PMC6722810/

20 Adrenal Glands. *John Hopkins Medicine.* Accessed Online September 5 2021. https://www.hopkinsmedicine.org/health/conditions-and-diseases /adrenal-glands

21 Eric G. Krause, Annette D. de Kloet, Jonathan N. Flak, Michael D. Smeltzer, Matia B. Solomon, Nathan K. Evanson, Stephen C. Woods, Randall R. Sakai and James P. Herman. Hydration State Controls Stress Responsiveness and Social Behavior. *Journal of Neuroscience.* April 6 2011 31(14): 5470-5476; DOI: https://doi.org/10.1523/ JNEUROSCI.6078-10.2011 online September 5 2021. https://www .jneurosci.org/content/31/14/5470

22 Banerjee N. Neurotransmitters in Alcoholism: A Review of Neurobiological and Genetic Studies. Indian J Hum Genet. 2014 20(1): 20–31. doi:10.4103/0971-6866.132750

23 Alcohol Use and Cancer. The American Cancer Society. Accessed online September 5 2021. https://www.cancer.org/cancer/cancer-causes/ diet-physical-activity/alcohol-use-and-cancer.html

24 Aldana, S. G., Sutton, L. D., Jacobson, B. H., and Quirk, M. G. (1996). Relationships between Leisure Time Physical Activity and Perceived Stress. Perceptual and Motor Skills. 82(1), 315–321. doi: 10.2466/ pms.1996.82.1.315

25 Fleshner, F. (2005). Physical Activity and Stress Resistance: Sympathetic Nervous System Adaptations Prevent Stress-Induced Immunosuppression. Exercise and Sport Sciences Reviews. 33(3), 120–126. doi: 10.1097/00003677-200507000-00004

26 Eric Suni. "Sleep Deprivation." Sleep Foundation. Accessed online April 16 2021. https://www.sleepfoundation.org/sleep-deprivation)

27 "Sleep Hygiene." Sleep Foundation. Accessed online July 1 2021. https:// www.sleepfoundation.org/sleep-hygiene

28 "Melatonin." National Sleep Foundation. Accessed July 1 2021. https:// www.sleepfoundation.org/melatonin

29 Zagajewski J, Drozdowicz D, Brzozowska I, Hubalewska-Mazgaj M,

Stelmaszynska T, Laidler PM, Brzozowski T. Conversion L-tryptophan to Melatonin in the Gastrointestinal Tract: The New High Performance Liquid Chromatography Method Enabling Simultaneous Determination of Six Metabolites of L-tryptophan by Native Fluorescence and UV-VIS Detection. *J Physiol Pharmacol.* 2012 December 63(6): 613–621. PMID: 23388477. Accessed online September 23 2021. https://pubmed.ncbi.nlm.nih.gov/23388477/

30 Birdsall TC. 5-Hydroxytryptophan: A Clinically-Effective Serotonin Precursor. *Altern Med Rev.* 1998 August 3(4): 271–280. PMID: 9727088. Accessed online September 23 2021. https://pubmed.ncbi.nlm.nih.gov/9727088/

31 Barbosa R, Scialfa JH, Terra IM, Cipolla-Neto J, Simonneaux V, Afeche SC. Tryptophan Hydroxylase Is Modulated by L-type Calcium Channels in the Rat Pineal Gland. *Life Sci.* 2008 February 27 82(9–10): 529–535. doi: 10.1016/j.lfs.2007.12.011. Epub 2007 December 23. PMID: 18221757. Accessed online September 23 2021. https://pubmed.ncbi.nlm.nih.gov/18221757/

32 "Vitamin B-6." National Institutes of Health Supplement Information For Healthcare Professionals. Accessed online September 23 2021. https://ods.od.nih.gov/factsheets/VitaminB6-HealthProfessional/

33 "Potassium." National Library of Medicine. Accessed online September 23 2021. https://medlineplus.gov/potassium.html

34 "Magnesium." National Institutes of Health Supplement Information For Healthcare Professionals. Accessed online September 23 2021. https://ods.od.nih.gov/factsheets/Magnesium-HealthProfessional/

35 "Napping: Do's and Don'ts For Healthy Adults." The Mayo Clinic. Accessed Online September 5 2021. https://www.mayoclinic.org/healthy-lifestyle/adult-health/in-depth/napping/art-20048319

36 "Stress Relief From Laughter: It's No joke." The Mayo Clinic. Accessed Online September 6 2021. https://www.mayoclinic.org/healthy-lifestyle/stress-management/in-depth/stress-relief/art-20044456